THE FUTURE OF
WOMEN'S WORK

NETWORK
FOUNDATION

Network Foundation for Educational Publishing is a voluntary foundation set up:

1. To facilitate the development of a healthy and responsible Canadian-controlled post-secondary book publishing sector.

2. To assist in the production, dissemination and popularizing of innovative texts and other educational materials for people at all levels of learning.

3. To develop more varied sources for critical works in the Humanities and Social Sciences.

4. to expand the readership for Canadian academic works beyond a select body of scholars.

5. To encourage the academic community to create books on Canadian topics for the community at large.

6. To develop works that will contribute to public information and debate on issues of historical and contemporary concern, thereby improving standards of education and public participation.

The Network Basics Series, one of the Foundation's activities, provides inexpensive books on the leading edge of research and debate to students and the general public.

This Network Basic is published by Garamond Press. Please direct all enquiries to 67A Portland Street, Toronto, Ontario, M5V 2M8.

The Canadian Centre for Policy Alternatives is an independent, non-profit research organization devoted to the development of progressive alternatives to current social and economic policies.

We recognize the need for viable, effective public policy, based on democratic control, public accountability, egalitarian principles and the right of our citizens to meaningful employment.

Membership is open to interested individuals and organizations; Centre members are encouraged to participate in voluntary research groups which undertake, supervise and co-ordinate research.

The Centre is governed by a Board of Directors, elected by the membership.

CANADIAN CENTRE FOR POLICY ALTERNATIVES, Suite 1004, 251 Laurier Avenue West, Ottawa, Ontario, K1P 5J6. (613) 563-1341.

FREE TRADE AND THE FUTURE OF WOMEN'S WORK:

Manufacturing and Service Industries

Marjorie Griffin Cohen

Garamond Press and the

Canadian Centre for Policy Alternatives

A NETWORK BASICS BOOK

A joint publication of Garamond Press and the Canadian Centre for Policy Alternatives.

Garamond Press
67A Portland Street
Toronto, Ontario M5V 2M9

Canadian Centre for Policy Alternatives
Suite 1004, 251 Laurier Avenue West
Ottawa, Ontario K1P 5J6

Cover design: Sharon Nelson
Typesetting: Coach House Press, Toronto

Printed and bound in Canada

Canadian Cataloguing in Publication Data

Cohen, Marjorie Griffin, 1944–.
    Free trade and the future of women's work

(Network basics series)
Co-published by the Canadian Centre for Policy Alternatives
Bibliography: p.
ISBN 0-920059-50-3   ISBN 0-88627-087-1

1. Foreign trade and employment – Canada. 2. Women – employment – Canada. 3. Service industries – Canada. 4. Canada – Manufactures. 5. Free trade and protection. 6. Tariff – Canada. I. Canadian Centre for Policy Alternatives. II. Title. III. Series.

HD5710.75.C3C64 1987   331.4'123'0971   C87-094714-1

Contents

List of Tables

Acknowledgements

The section on the service sector was originally prepared as a background paper for the Canadian Advisory Council on the Status of Women. Many people were helpful to me at various stages in the preparation of this study, but I would particularly like to thank Doug Cunningham and Susan Turner for their help in gathering information and Melody Mason-Richmond and Ted Richmond for their editorial work. I also appreciate the enthusiastic support I have received from Errol Sharpe and Sharon Nelson at Garamond Press and Peter Findlay at the Canadian Centre for Policy Alternatives.

The societies that achieved the most spectacular broad-based economic progress in the shortest period of time have not been the biggest in size, nor the richest in resources and certainly not the most rigidly controlled. What has united them all was their belief in the magic of the market.

> *— Ronald Reagan, Speech to the Board of Governors of the International Monetary Fund/World Bank Group annual meeting, 1983.*

It [the bourgeoisie] has resolved personal worth into exchange value and in place of the numberless indefeasible chartered freedoms, has set up that single unconscionable freedom – Free Trade.

> *— Karl Marx, The Communist Manifesto*

Introduction

Recently on a trip to Mexico I happened to find in my hotel room a copy of an AFL-CIO magazine which had an article on free trade written by its president, Lane Kirkland. With some effort I overcame the paranoid feeling that there was an "invisible hand" directing every facet of my life towards this issue: I forced myself to read the article. What is remarkable about it (and the reason I raise it now) is not that Kirkland is against free trade – labour leaders on both sides of the border recognize its dangers – but his reasons for opposing it. His complaint is that most of the world disavows a private market economy:

> There are no open markets among our trade partners ... not unless "free and open markets" means import quotas, discriminatory performance and inspection requirements, export subsidies and incentives, industrial targeting programs, controlled currency exchange rates, and barter agreements.[1]

Kirkland's perspective is significant because it points to the crucial differences in beliefs about what is right and wrong about the way countries should manage their economic and social policies. In the United States there is little recognition of the fact that vast differences in the circumstances of countries demand different ways of solving

11

problems. Their demand is that we all do things their way: if we do not, we are accused of unfair trading practices. With free trade Canada will be forced to harmonize social and economic policies so that they conform to those of the United States

In Canada the debate over free trade is a debate about the nature of change in our society. For the most part the arguments have been structured around whether free trade will be good or bad for the economy. This is important, but the argument cannot be won or lost simply by an appeal to economic logic for there is much more at stake than whether business will prosper or decline because of it. The issue is fundamentally about the future – about the values and moral standards of Canadians. What we are arguing about is not simply how to achieve "the good life," but essentially what it is that makes life good. We're fighting about the objectives of this country and the ways to achieve these objectives. For this reason free trade is a tremendously divisive issue. To some it is strange that free trade is able to arouse such strong political passion in this country. But there are good reasons why it does so: more than any other public issue, free trade dramatizes the very different interests dividing ordinary people and the rich and powerful.

Those who argue in favour of free trade have a long tradition behind them. The basic ideas of orthodox economics teach that the most efficient, productive society is one where individuals are free to pursue their own self-interest through the private market. The private market, through the price mechanism, is best able to sort out the wants, desires, abilities, and needs of individuals if it is not unduly restricted by regulation, manipulation, and government interference. There is a happy coincidence in this view of the individual pursuit of self-interest – it also benefits society as a whole. In the famous words of Adam Smith, the individual is

> Led by an invisible hand to promote an end which was no part of his intention ... By pursuing his own interest he frequently promotes that of the society more effectually than when he really intends to promote it.[2]

While Adam Smith qualified his words by saying "frequently," rather than invariably, the belief that the private market mechanism can, in an inadvertent way, look after the interests of society better than deliberate policy and effort, has been elevated to a theology over the centuries.

Ronald Reagan refers to the "belief in the magic of the market" and the *Globe and Mail* in its editorial "The Scale of Value" (July 10, 1985) to the "genius of the market" in an attempt to convince people that returning to a more pure market-oriented economy would be the best solution to economic and social problems. The general argument put forward by public officials and many economists is that a proliferation of government programs and regulations distorts the rational operation of supply and demand as the regulators of production and distribution and this is why the economy does not function properly. In particular they point to marketing boards, transportation and communication regulations, unemployment insurance, government subsidies to business, international trade restrictions, government ownership of key industries, and various forms of labour legislation as obstacles which prevent the price mechanism from working properly. The solution, as they see it, is to dismantle these barriers. The major initiatives in this direction are free trade, privatization, and deregulation. But free trade is the over-riding vehicle for accomplishing dramatic changes in social policy and for reducing or eliminating the programs and activities which "distort" the market. These changes will be accomplished in indirect ways, to be elaborated on later, which will make it possible for the government to avoid politically unpopular actions. The promise is that the short-term pain associated with the inevitable restructuring of the economy will be compensated for by long-term gain.

My major objection to the strategy of greater reliance on market forces is that it is based on a utopian notion of the power of the market. Experience has certainly shown us that the market is not sufficiently sensitive to human needs and wants that it automatically adjusts to do the fair and correct thing. In fact, it cannot even be relied upon to self-adjust when market failure itself occurs. When unemployment levels are astronomically high, as during the great depression, only human intervention (in the form of war or planned activity) breaks the dismal pattern. When gross inequalities in income distribution or discrinination against certain groups occur, the private market simply cannot compensate. Because of the pitifully slow pace of market adjustment, almost as soon as the private market was recognized as the dominant force in production and distribution decisions, there were attempts to limit the damage it caused to people: its raw power was simply too brutal to be tolerated. So, way back when capitalism was just a glimmer in the mercantilist's eye, poor laws were introduced because the market could not provide everyone with a living wage. As factories developed, legislation to protect workers against gross exploitation by employers was necessary. Society could not live with the assumption that "in the long run" everything would turn out well, and that employers would recognize the value of conserving human lives: it was too obvious that lives were being destroyed in the short run.

Over time the market has been humanized. We know that business, by quietly and confidently pursuing its own self interest, does *not* usually benefit the whole of society. In practice we have recognized the limits of the private market, but in the dominant ideology and in economic theory we are still very dependent on the abstract notion of how it works to guide our actions. What is particularly worrying now is that as governments become increasingly bankrupt of ideas about how to solve economic and social problems they find the laissez-faire ideal more compelling. I think it is particularly attractive to them because when things go wrong no one can point to government action and say – you did the wrong thing. Rather, the market can be blamed and problems can be viewed as part of a normal adjustment phase.

The moves toward free trade, privatization, and deregulation are part of an ideological package. We tend to talk about them separately, but they are all part of a vast global restructuring which will give greater capital mobility to giant firms. In Canada we are told that with less government interference and free trade, business will reorganize and become more rational. Small, inefficient firms will fail but strong healthy ones will survive, and ultimately, given enough time (the economist's favourite caveat), everyone will be better off. But the real financial and personal costs to people, in terms of unemployment, wage rates, quality of work and provision of social services, have been grossly neglected in the calculations these changes will bring.

It certainly is in the interests of big business to be able to shift production to wherever costs are lowest. But this is not usually in the best interest of nations or of the people in them. Somehow the notion of free competition seems fair, but the relative power between big business and workers is not comparable – and labour certainly is not as mobile as capital and will not ever be, even with free trade. There will always be someplace in the world where wages are lower than the subsistence level here; there will always be someplace where governments are more repressive and therefore able to provide a more "attractive" business environment; there will always be someplace where working conditions are worse. Yet the notion that workers in Canada must get used to a lower standard of living and lower wages is the heart of the argument for a truly free market. People are told that we must become more "adaptable" so that Canadian business can become more competitive.

* * *

My intent in this study is to show why women's jobs are particularly vulnerable under a free trade agreement. I do not mean to imply that free trade is invariably bad for women in all circumstances. There have been times in our history when the most lucrative work for women was hindered by trade restrictions. In the 1830s, Harriet Martineau was particularly scathing about the prohibition against free traffic in butter and eggs between the United States and Canada because of the difficulties it presented for women. She wrote of a woman in Canada who told her how the women in her neighborhood were forced to become smugglers in order to sell their wares in Buffalo.[3]

But whether free trade is good or bad for a nation (or for women) has little to do with the idea in the abstract – the concrete circumstances of the time have to be considered. What may be good under one set of conditions may be disastrous under another. Considering the current structure of the Canadian economy and the industries which will be adversely affected by free trade, women will be the major losers in a bilateral free-trade deal with the United States.

In this study I begin by examining the five manufacturing industries which are the biggest employers of women. Over 60 per cent of the women working in manufacturing industries are employed in textiles, clothing, food processing, electrical and electronic products, and leather products. Generally it is conceded, even by promoters of free trade, that considerable restructuring of manufacturing industries will occur as a result of a free-trade agreement with the United States. But the most optimistic supporters do not anticipate radical shifts between industries. Rather, they predict "intra-industry" restructuring of production.[4] This means no industries will experience serious declines, but will gradually reorganize production to find their "niche" in international markets. I dispute this view and show that in some industries which are major employers of women there will be serious production and job losses. But even within those industries which do manage to find the proper "niche" in international trade, the focus will be on shifting production away from those areas within the industry where women work. The result, then, will be a significant decline in women's jobs in the manufacturing sector. This will accelerate the trend for women's work to shift away from the manufacturing sector toward more service-type jobs. For the manufacturing jobs which remain, there will be strong pressures to reduce wages and limit the power of trade unions. Firms facing particularly stiff American competition will be forced to reduce costs by lower wages and by providing fewer benefits to workers. They will undoubtedly become even more strident in their opposition to labour legislation which is directed toward improving the bargaining strength of unions and correcting the wage gap between males and females.

In the second part of this study I examine some of the major issues regarding free trade in services. This is of particular importance to women because the vast majority of working women are employed in the service sector. I argue that although the impact of free trade on the service sector has received little attention in the debate, it is the most important item for the United States. Several issues are of paramount importance to those working in the service sector in Canada. A general agreement on free trade in services may mean substantial job loss in those areas where services could be provided from outside the country. The areas of particular concern here are data processing, financial services, communications, transportation and cultural industries. But in other areas, the importing of services is less significant than the guarantee of access to the Canadian market for American service firms which locate in this country. Of crucial importance then are the negotiations over right of establishment and right of national treatment. American firms want to be able to operate in Canada and not be disadvantaged because they do not receive the same treatment as their competitors. A free trade agreement which enforces the right of establishment and right of national treatment may have considerable impact on the way certain services, such as day care and health services, are provided. I argue that there will be strong forces which will compel these services to be increasingly privatized. This will affect the availability of many services and the conditions of work for those employed in the industries.

This study is a response to the government's lack of concern about what free trade will mean for women. The initiative to negotiate free trade with the United States began because of pressure from big business. Canada rushed into it without public debate and without a clear understanding of what it will mean for people. This study is not comprehensive in that I have not been able to cover all industries and all occupations in which women's work is threatened by a free trade arrangement. The discussion of the manufacturing sector is fairly detailed because information about specific industries is readily available. However, this is not the case with the discussion of the service sector. In this area the information is scanty and the consequences of free trade much less direct. But I try to focus on the industries which seem most at risk to show the complex array of factors which will affect these industries. I have not tried to calculate how many women's jobs will be lost. This cannot be done now because so much will depend on the exact nature of the agreement which is negotiated. In some sectors, particularly in manufacturing, the impact will occur in a fairly short period of time. However, in others, such as in the public services, changes will be more gradual and will change in response to the necessity to harmonize social policy over a fairly long period of time.

While free trade with the United States is the focus of this study the implications of the results of trade liberalization are not confined to our relations with this country. There are compelling forces at work to liberalize trade throughout the world. In the upcoming negotiations of the Uruguay Round of the General Agreement on Tariffs and Trade (GATT) the same issues will be debated as are now being raised in bilateral negotiations. For the United States successful negotiations with Canada are important because they will strengthen their position in multilateral negotiations, particularly in areas where the United States has met considerable opposition in the past – most notably areas such as trade in services, procurement, intellectual property rights, and foreign investment. An executive of American Express recently stated it quite explicitly:

> We can achieve more bilaterally than we can currently hope for in the new round [of GATT] – which means that an early and comprehensive U.S.-Canada agreement could serve as a goad to other countries, forcing them to reevaluate their positions on liberalization.[5]

What Canada has to decide is whether trade-led growth is the best path for the future of this country and whether trade policy should direct economic goals or serve them. With a commitment to free trade Canadians will have less ability to determine their own future – it will be determined by the blind forces of the market. The question at stake with free trade is whether government policy will meet the demands of the people of this country or the demands of business. These are different objectives and cannot be met by the same policies.

Part One

Free Trade and Women's Employment in Manufacturing

There is a strange contradiction in the government's perception of what the impact of free trade will be on women's jobs in the manufacturing sector. On the most general level there is a willingness to admit that the manufacturing industries where women are concentrated are among the more vulnerable industries in trade liberalization. The Macdonald Commission report, for example, lists textiles, clothing, footwear, electrical products and consumer goods as among the weakest industries in secondary manufacturing.[1] These are industries where there are particularly high concentrations of female workers. Although women account for only 25 per cent of all workers in manufacturing, they make up about 80 per cent of workers in clothing industries, 40 per cent in textiles, 65 per cent in footwear, 38 per cent in electrical products and over 30 per cent in food processing (Table 1). That is, the industries in which women are most heavily concentrated are the most threatened by free trade.

But what is odd is that the government is making projections about the restructuring of the labour force as a result of free trade based on a study which sees textiles, clothing, and related industries as the *growth* areas in employment. In a massive project which is establishing an "adjustment" policy for Canada, the trade model of Richard Harris and David Cox is being used to indicate which industries will expand and which will contract under free trade. The strange findings of the Harris and Cox model are that textiles, clothing, knitting, and transportation equipment are going to be the industries to provide the greatest increases in jobs. In their study of the effect of bilateral free trade Harris and Cox estimate that employment will increase by a staggering 260 per cent in the clothing industry, 156 per cent in textiles, and 48 per cent in knitting. Production in clothing will rise by 480 per cent, in textiles by 240 per cent, and in knitting by over 100 per cent.[2]

The problem with these predictions is that they fly in the face of sectoral studies which have looked specifically at the prospects for these industries in the light of trade liberalization. Harris and Cox's predictions also ignore what has happened to employment in these industries in the past when trade restrictions were indisputably inadequate. Considering that about one-third of the female manufacturing labour force is engaged in the textile and clothing industries, and about two-thirds are working in industries identified as weak and "vulnerable", it is important that the employment predictions be accurate.

In what follows I look at the five manufacturing industries which account for over 60 per cent of women's jobs in the manufacturing sector. These are textiles, clothing, food processing, electrical and electronic products and leather products. Only about 12 per cent of working women in Canada are employed in manufacturing, but a free-trade agreement with the United States could radically restructure women's labour force experience and reduce this proportion considerably. Specifically I show that free trade will increase women's unemployment, will confine women's work to an even more narrow range of occupations, and will adversely affect the ability of women to pursue better working conditions through unionization. It is also likely that the wage gap between males and females will grow and that competitive pressures will inhibit the effective use of social policies to correct the labour market inequalities between males and females.

Prospects for the Textile and Clothing Industries

The debate over whether textiles and clothing are "sunset" industries [i.e., that their demise is inevitable because of competition from low-wage countries] is considerably clouded by studies like that of Harris and Cox. Of course, whether they can survive in the face of imports from the Pacific Rim countries is quite a different matter from how they will fare with regard to free trade with the United States. Nevertheless, the ability of these industries to maintain their strength is of considerable importance to the Canadian economy. They are the second largest industrial employers in Canada, employing 12 per cent of the

Table 1
Employment Structure in Major Manufacturing Groups

	Total Employment	Males	Females	Females as % of total
All manufacturing	1,193,584	900,025	292,760	25%
Food industries	129,301	88,949	40,352	31%
Beverage	17,071	15,727	1,344	8%
Tobacco	4,955	3,009	1,935	39%
Rubber	17,577	15,370	2,187	12%
Plastics	25,011	17,012	7,999	32%
Leather	20,397	8,132	12,265	60%
(Footwear)	(14,465)	(5,101)	(9,364)	(65%)
Textiles	47,508	28,517	18,991	40%
Clothing	96,636	20,639	75,997	79%
Wood	85,499	80,357	5,142	6%
Furniture	35,702	29,044	6,658	19%
Transport equipment	130,847	112,883	17,964	14%
Electrical & electronic products	78,636	48,798	29,838	38%
Non-metallic mineral products	34,097	31,349	2,748	8%
Refined petroleum & coal products	7,417	7,276	141	2%
Chemical & Chem products	46,084	36,117	9,967	22%

Source: Statistics Canada. *Manufacturing Industries of Canada: National and Provincial Areas* 1983. April 1986.

manufacturing labour force; only the food and beverage industrial group employs slightly more. The level of production is significant as well since it accounts for about 7 per cent of the Gross Domestic Product (GDP).[3] The point is that any restructuring of these industries through new trade arrangements will have a considerable impact on a large number of workers and on the level of production in the economy.

However significant the textile and clothing industries are to economic performance and the level of employment in this country, it is clear that domestic consumption is the focus of production: these

Table 2
Canada: Imports and Exports of Textile and
Clothing Products (in thousand Canadian dollars)

	1979	1983	1985
Imports			
Apparel	828,507	1,292,623	1,804,423
Textiles	1,332,796	1,482,640	1,885,529
Total	2,161,303	2,775,263	3,689,952
Exports			
Apparel	180,236	223,554	332,362
Textiles	165,527	227,223	283,269
Total	345,763	450,777	615,631
Trade Deficit	$1.8 billion	$2.3 billion	$3.1 billion

Sources: Statistics Canada, *Summary of Canadian International Trade,* December 1985.

industries are not major exporters. In fact, the trade deficit in textiles and clothing is large and is growing year by year. In 1979 it was $1.8 billion – by 1985 it had grown to $3.1 billion (Table 2).

Canadians spend more per capita on clothing and textile imports than almost any other industrialized country (with the exception of Sweden, which has more or less abandoned production in these areas).[4] In both textiles and clothing the proportion of Canadian consumption provided by domestic production has decreased dramatically in recent years. While textile imports accounted for 55 per cent of the Canadian market in 1980, they had increased to 60 per cent by 1984. But apparel imports have grown at an even more staggering rate. In 1981 domestic production accounted for almost 70 per cent of the Canadian market, but by 1984 had dropped to less than 60 per cent.[5]

In spite of the general trend toward trade liberalization in traded goods under GATT, industrialized countries have gone to great lengths to exclude textiles and clothing from freer trade arrangements. This is because of the considerable importance these industries still hold for the general level of economic activity and employment for western nations. Most industrialized countries feel a need to protect these industries from the tremendous disruption which would occur from unrestrained imports from low-wage countries. Since 1974 the textiles and clothing trade has been regulated by an agreement known as the Multi-Fibre Arrangement (MFA). This agreement permits countries to restrict imports through quotas and tariffs if imports are causing market disruptions.[6] What is particularly interesting is that Canada's policy in this area was comparatively liberal in the early 1970s, but there were some rather disastrous consequences which forced Canada to adopt more stringent measures to protect domestic industry. Competition from new suppliers in low-cost countries became increasingly harmful, particularly in light of the appreciation of the Canadian dollar in 1976. From 1971 to 1976 domestic clothing producers' share of the Canadian market dropped from 73 per cent to 55 per cent. During the same period employment in clothing dropped by 20,000 jobs and in textiles by 12,000 jobs.[7] It became clear that Canada was more vulnerable to import competition than other industrialized countries. The result was the introduction of more stringent protective measures than existed.

The United States also has restrictions on clothing and textile imports, but their belief is that restrictions should be limited to low-cost suppliers; i.e., state-trading countries or any other nations which have a substantial cost advantage because of low wage costs.[8] So, essentially, the United States favours free trade in textiles and clothing between developed countries. In fact, American producers would have a great deal to gain should free trade with Canada become a reality. The real fear in a bilateral free trade agreement is that the Canadian domestic market will be seriously eroded. The ability of United States firms to penetrate the Canadian market (as a result of marketing and cost advantages) is much stronger than the ability of Canadian firms to make inroads in the American market. In fact, the American industry is one of the most efficient producers of textiles in the world primarily because it is relatively capital-intensive and technologically advanced. As a result of fairly cheap fabric inputs, its clothing industry is stronger than its Canadian counterpart, and better able to compete with imports from low-wage countries.

American textile imports are considerably more significant for Canada than are apparel imports. While about 60 per cent of the textile imports are from the United States, only about 10 per cent of our clothing imports are from there. The major competition for clothing manufacturers is from importers in low-wage countries of the Pacific Rim. On the surface it would appear, then, that Canada has fairly little to lose – at least as regards clothing imports – in a bilateral free trade arrangement with the United States. However, this is not quite the case.

A 1984 study of the Textile and Clothing Board indicates that while Canadian clothing exporters do reasonably well in selling high priced products, the Canadian portion of the United States market is very small and is disadvantaged relative to their American competition because of the much larger production runs there, enabling producers to benefit from lower costs.[9] Although some export expansion in high priced clothing is considered likely, this is not expected to be a dramatic change over current conditions.

One serious problem which the Textile and Clothing Board warns against is the very real possibility that with free trade, and the removal of the necessity to produce in Canada in order to sell substantial quantities of clothing here, domestic production will decrease. This would occur in part because at the moment many holders of United States trade marks would take back the exclusive use of their trade mark and would terminate their licencing agreements with Canadian producers.[10] Similarly, designers in other countries could withdraw their licencing agreements with Canadian manufacturers and simply import from their suppliers in the United States. The 1984 Textile and Clothing Board study argues that actions of this sort could have a serious effect on the manufacture of clothing here. So, although the United States is not a major source of import competition in clothing at the present time, this would very likely change with free trade.

In textiles the threat of American competition is even clearer. The American textile industry is eleven times larger than the Canadian and is much better placed to take advantage of economies of scale. The Canadian Textile Institute estimates that a 5 per cent increase in American production would be enough to supply the entire Canadian market. This could be accomplished fairly easily without any added investment since firms there are now operating considerably below capacity.[11] Currently Canadian textile exports to the United States are confined to basic products – there is little specialization primarily because of the inability to produce long production runs in a wide variety of materials. The result is that the textiles trade deficit with the United States ($1.6 billion in 1985) is enormous. According to the Textile and Clothing Board while certain sectors, like the wool industry, may benefit from free trade, others would be considerably worse off. Those which would suffer most would be the cotton and polyester industries and the "man-made" yarn and fabric industries.

One of the major problems the Board anticipates is the gradual shift of existing production to the United States. While the Canadian textile industry does not lag behind the United States in production technology, it does not have a comparative advantage because it has higher production costs. While wage rates are similar in the two countries, construction costs are much higher in Canada than in the "sun belt" states. Also, the relatively low value of the Canadian dollar and the necessity to import the technology needed to modernize are factors which place Canadian firms at a cost disadvantage. In some parts of the industry, particularly the artificial fibre sector, there is a high degree of foreign ownership and the tendency to eliminate Canadian subsidiaries could be strong. But whether industries are Canadian or American owned, there are considerable inducements for relocation in southeastern and southwestern states. These states are considered choice geographical locations for both textile and clothing producers because of the large pool of labour available, low wages, lower start-up costs and favourable government regulations and labour relations.[12]

Not all manufacturers would be affected in the same way. For those which have already moved some of their production out of the country, free trade is not a threat. However, for those whose production takes place entirely in Canada, the reorganization and relocation as a result of free trade will be considerable. For example, the president of Stanfield's Ltd. of Truro, Nova Scotia, has warned that the company's manufacturing operations may be forced out of the country by a freer trade deal with the United States. This would mean that about 90 per cent of the company's 800 jobs would be lost to this country.[13]

Another serious problem for the textile industry arises because of its dependence on the strength of the domestic clothing industry. The clothing industry is the textile industry's largest customer, therefore, as domestic apparel production is eroded by import competition (garment imports increased by 43 per cent from 1982-84) markets for textiles decrease.[14] The Canadian Textile Institute feels this is the major factor contributing to the decline in the textile industry's share of the domestic market in recent years.

Food Processing

The food processing industry is another which is considerably threatened by the prospect of a bilateral free-trade agreement with the United States. The damage anticipated will affect almost all areas of production and the near unanimity amongst manufacturers on this issue reflects the extent of the fears: all the major associations of food processing manufacturers have cautioned the government against proceeding with negotiations until fundamental changes in the Canadian economy have been made. They feel that not only is Canada's industry ill-equipped to expand exports, but that the very existence of production for the domestic market is threatened by free trade.[15]

While most food processing industries predict serious losses in production and employment levels, those areas where women work are considered to be least able to compete with American imports. This will have serious consequences for women in the manufacturing sector since about one-seventh of all women working in this sector are employed in food processing. After textiles and clothing, this is the second most important manufacturing employer for women. Within the food processing industrial grouping women's employment is concentrated in six areas which possess 87 per cent of all women working in this sector: the processing of fish, bakery goods, sugar and confectionaries, fruit and vegetables, poultry, and meat.

Food processing in Canada is generally disadvantaged relative to production in the United States because of higher costs, most of which are unavoidable and have relatively little to do with problems of efficiency. Canada possesses a size and a climate which makes domestic production precarious unless there is considerable protection from imports. In comparison with producers in the United States, we have a much shorter growing season, lower population densities, greater distances over which raw materials and finished products must be transported, and higher construction and energy costs. The industry's producers also feel they are disadvantaged because of other conditions not solely related to geographic problems: these are labour costs which are routinely higher than those in the United States, higher costs of raw materials because of the supply-management powers of marketing boards, and regulated transportation costs.[16]

Most production is geared toward the domestic market; however, the domestic market itself has been eroded by import competition. Growth in imports has been greatest in areas where women's employment in the industry is significant; i.e., in fruit and vegetables, confectionary, and biscuit products. Exports have remained fairly stable, but they are concentrated in only a few product categories, such as fish and meat. According to the Grocery Products Manufacturers of Canada, the food industry is "only competitive in world markets in some raw commodities and semi-processed natural products".[17] In recent years there has been considerable consolidation of production within the industry. For example, now there are about half the number of fruit and vegetable processing establishments than there were twenty-five years ago. This is partially a reflection of the growth of multinational firms in the Canadian market. While Canadian firms account for about 70 per cent of all the food processing firms in Canada, the bulk of production capacity – a full two-thirds – is owned by foreign manufacturers.[18] What this means is that the Canadian firms tend to be small. Since Canadian subsidiaries of many multinational food processing concerns were

Table 3
Female Labour Concentration
in Food Processing Industries

Industry	Number employed	% of workers in industry
Fish products	10,163	48%
Bakery products	6,111	34%
Sugar & sugar confectionary	5,293	44%
Fruit and vegetables	4,901	39%
Poultry products	4,276	52%
Meat & meat products	4,250	17%
Total food industry	40,342	31%

Source: Statistics Canada, *Manufacturing Industries of Canada: National and Provincial Areas*, 1983 (Ottawa, April 1986).

established here to circumvent tariff barriers, it is feared that the dismantling of trade barriers will result in shifts in production to the United States and serious job losses in Canada.

While all sectors of the food processing industry feel threatened by the prospect of free trade, the processing related to horticulture and supply-managed commodities are considered to be particularly at a disadvantage. Women's employment would be affected especially in fruit and vegetable processing and in the preparation of poultry products. In the processing of fruit and vegetable products the geographical disadvantages are considerable. Free trade would permit American industries to service the Canadian market all year round. This is a market which has had the highest protection and therefore is least likely to survive under free trade. This is so because American industry is better able to realize economies of scale and could easily supply the Canadian market without a significant increase in investment. The problems in the poultry industry are similar. This industry is highly regulated and quotas on imports have protected the domestic market to a great degree. The removal of import quotas will result in a flood of imports from the United States; producers there are in a much better position to realize economies of scale. The result will be drastically lower consumer prices but also a sharp reduction in production in

Canada. According to a study prepared by Deloitte Haskins and Sells, the Canadian industry could not operate competitively in an unregulated international market. They are adamant that the poultry industry should be exempt from any free-trade arrangement on the grounds that the industry simply could not survive.[19]

Two areas of food processing which appear to be best able to tolerate a move toward free trade are fish and meat products. Women account for almost half of the workers in fish processing (more than 60 per cent in fish processing in BC) but less than 20 per cent of the meat processors. However, in both of these industries the tendency is for Canada to export unfinished or "crude" products and to import the more processed items.[20] While it is hoped that complete free trade in these items would mean that Canada could increase value-added exports, the likelihood of this happening (and of processing jobs in these areas expanding) is small. United States fish processing firms are large and can effectively keep Canadian firms out of the market. The same problem exists for the meat industry: the Canadian Meat Council feels that the American industry has decided that Canada's share of the North American market should not expand further and will press for the increased use of trade remedy legislation to keep Canadian products out. They also worry about the advantages of economies of scale for American firms: a plant in Iowa can draw on more hogs produced in that state than a Canadian plant can reach in all of Canada.

The effect of free trade on food processing will be immediate and will have repercussions in other sectors of the economy. The Canadian Food Processors Association estimates that twenty plants will close and production will become more concentrated in a few large plants. This would mean an immediate loss of many product lines and about 3,000 full-time jobs. In particular, Canada would cease to be self-sufficient in a number of fruit and vegetable commodities. Industries which supply goods and services to the food processing sector would experience loss of markets and a substantial amount of acreage would be taken out of cultivation. For many small communities which depend heavily on seasonal farming income there would be heavy losses.[21]

The loss of employment in the food processing sector would affect women in manufacturing across Canada because the industry is regionally dispersed with plants located in every province. While the greatest proportion of workers in this industry are located in Ontario, the industry accounts for a high proportion of total manufacturing employment in the Eastern and Prairie provinces. Unlike manufacturing in general, employment in this industry is relatively evenly distributed throughout the country in proportion to population densities.

Electrical and Electronic Products

The production of electrical and electronic products accounts for about 10 per cent of women's labour in the manufacturing sector. The effect of free trade on this industrial grouping is likely to be uneven, with some types of production expanding while others contract substantially. However, the industries where women's labour is concentrated are most likely to suffer adversely.

Almost half of the women in this industrial group are employed in manufacturing electronic products. This industry has substantial appeal in development programs because of its promise as a high-technology industry that is expanding rapidly on a global basis. However, Canada is not in the forefront of this worldwide explosion, rather, electronics is, as one analyst put it, "a niche-oriented sector, where the Canadian industry has no broad capabilities."[22] The perspective of specific firms within the industry on the effect of free trade depends substantially on their size and whether they are foreign or domestic firms. The tendency throughout the industry is for large, American owned firms to favour a bilateral free trade agreement while small Canadian owned firms do not.[23] Foreign ownership dominates the electronics sector. While most firms are Canadian owned (80 per cent) the foreign-owned firms account for 55 per cent of the industry's sales.[24]

Employment within the electronics industries tends to be highly skewed. This industry is the largest industrial employer of scientific and technical personnel in Canada, most of whom are men. The majority of female workers are found in low-skilled manufacturing jobs. The labour profile of the industry has not been static: it has been shifting away from concentration in manufacturing towards a large proportion of information specialists such as engineers and computer programmers – free trade is likely to accelerate this trend. Because of the high rate of business formation, workers in this field tend not to be unionized and therefore are felt to be more vulnerable to the labour shifts which will result from free trade. Essentially labour in the manufacturing parts of the sector is considered to be the most likely target in the reorganization of the industry through free trade.[25] The industries least able to withstand the increased competition free trade would bring will be those manufacturing consumer electrical and electronic components. But also it is feared that, in general, investment will tend to flow south when the Canadian market can be easily serviced from production there.

The electrical products industry in Canada is a much more mature industry than the electronics industry. As a result, its labour force is highly unionized. Nevertheless, this is not likely to be sufficient protection for workers, as production would be rationalized on a global basis as a result of free trade. Those favouring free trade expect that firms which had been established in Canada to serve the Canadian market by providing the company's whole range of consumer products would reorganize production to specialize in specific products. They feel that this would increase both efficiency and exports. The large multinational firms in this industry favour free trade because it would, in fact, facilitate the reorganization of production without sacrificing access to the Canadian market. But what is good for these large firms is likely to benefit labour very little: rationalization may mean simply less production and employment in Canada.

The case of Canadian General Electric (CGE) is a good example of how things can go wrong. For many years most of the small appliances which Canadians bought were made in Canada. The CGE plant in Barrie, Ontario, the largest in the country, made twenty-six small appliances until it was given the world product mandate for seven items. Production for the remaining products was moved to the United States and other GE factories around the world. In the reorganization of production the labour force at the Barrie factory dropped from 1,100 to 450.[26] Ultimately CGE eliminated its operation in Canada altogether when it sold its operations to Black and Decker; the Barrie plant was closed.

The outlook for small Canadian firms is fairly bleak. The Electrical and Electronic Manufacturers Association of Canada anticipates that many segments of the industry will be wiped out. Although the multinational firms favour free trade, the extent to which they would continue using Canadian facilities in their rationalization plans is uncertain. One fairly clear development, however, would be the exaggeration of regional concentration in central Canada. Currently the effect of certain provincial trade barriers, including government procurement policies, has meant that production has been widely dispersed. With free trade it is expected that these barriers will be removed and rationalization of production will mean the closing of many small regional operations.[27]

Footwear

The footwear industry has been considerably damaged by import competition in recent years: domestic producers manage to supply only about half of the total Canadian market.[28] To give some measure of protection to domestic production the government began to impose quotas on imports in 1977. By 1981 import quotas were lifted, but since the result was a substantial increase in imports and a significant decline in Canadian production, the quotas on leather footwear were reimposed. However, quotas are once again being phased out. The first to be lifted were those for men's and children's shoes. The impact on production and employment have been dramatic. In a fourteen-month period shoe production in Canada dropped and almost 1,500 shoe workers lost their jobs. During the same period the average price for imported children's footwear increased by 26 per cent and for men's imported shoes by 7 per cent.[29] The government had predicted that shoe prices would drop when import quotas were lifted. The production of women's shoes is still protected by quotas, but these will be lifted by 1988. Tariffs in excess of 23 per cent continue to give this industry considerable protection from imports.

The major import competition comes from Taiwan and South Korea. These two countries account for almost 55 per cent of all imported footwear. Italy is the third most important source of imports, but unlike the imports from the far east, which provide low-cost items, Italy supplies the high-quality, high cost leather shoes. Between 1980 and 1984 American imports to Canada dropped from being the fourth most important source of footwear imports to the seventh. It now provides about one-third fewer pairs of shoes and boots than it did four years ago.[30]

Women make up the majority of workers (65 per cent) in the footwear industry. It is an industry which is almost entirely confined to central Canada: about 60 per cent of the industry's labour force is located in Ontario and 37 per cent is in Quebec. Ontario employs a larger proportion of women than the industry does in Quebec. This is probably a result of the differences in the location of industries: in Ontario factories tend to be located in cities while in Quebec more firms are located in smaller communities where families are employed. While generally the industry has managed to perform well compared to other industries within the goods producing sector during the past twelve years, there has been erosion of the strength of the labour force: from 1974-1983 there has been an over-all decline of about 11 per cent. Almost all of these losses occurred in Quebec.[31]

While the stated objective of free trade, according to the government, is to force the reorganization of production so that economies of scale can be realized and exports can be increased, a bilateral free trade agreement with the United States will have little effect on the export potential of the Canadian industry. At the moment there are relatively few trade barriers which prevent Canadian access to the American market: the United States has a much lower tariff than does Canada (8 per cent) and does not impose import quotas. Canadian producers have little chance of increasing their penetration of the United States market both because of the competition from American firms and from competition of low-cost imports from Taiwan, Korea, and Brazil. Even American producers are hard hit by these imports, which now account for almost three-quarters of all shoe sales there.[32] The major effect of the bilateral agreement for the Canadian industry, according to Canadian producers, will be increased competition in the Canadian market, particularly for smaller firms which are already facing fierce competition from low-wage countries.[33]

Gains or Losses?

Despite the fairly clear indication that a portion of the manufacturing industries most important for women's employment will be in serious difficulty as a result of free trade, there are always those who have something to gain by free trade within each industry. It is these interests that the government highlights in trying to create the impression that there is a " mixed reaction by business." For example, Peter Nygard, head of Tan Jay, is the government's trump card in showing how "divided" textile and clothing entrepreneurs are about the effect free trade will have on the industry and it is people like him who have been appointed to head the government's advisory groups on trade. However, it must be pointed out that Nygard's operation is in a class by itself. Over a short period of time his firm benefited greatly from government subsidies. While only a limited amount of data was available, that which was uncovered revealed that from 1977 to 1983 he received at least $5.6 million in public funds.[34] As a result of being on the public dole at the rate of about a million dollars a year his operations grew considerably. In fact, Tan Jay expanded to such an extent that Nygard has been able to shift production from Canada (where he was facing worker opposition to his poor employment policies) to low-wage countries off-shore. Small wonder, then, that Peter Nygard favours relaxing import restrictions: he's leaving Canada but wants to maintain access to the market here. Having someone like Nygard around is eminently convenient for the government. He is used again and again as an example of an entrepreneur in a "vulnerable" industry who has "made it" and who favours the government position.

It is difficult to put a figure on the numbers of workers likely to experience job loss in each industry. So much depends on just what degree of trade liberalization takes place, what kinds of provisions are made for adjustments considering Canada's weaker position, and the length of time allowed for the phasing-out of import restrictions.

Table 4
Labour Force Tracking Data
(1974-76 Separations)

Industry	Left Labour Force (%)	Unemployed at time of Survey (%)
Clothing		
Male	13	10
Female	29	21
Primary Textiles		
Male	12	15
Female	25	28
Electronics and Electrical		
Male	11	15
Female	21	41

Source: Canada. Department of Industry, Trade and Commerce, *A Report on the Labour Force Tracking Project/Cost of Labour Adjustment Study* (Ottawa, March 1979) Tables 3, 6.

Certainly even with the total removal of protection of the domestic industries, some "remnants" of production will remain.

We do have indications from the experience in the mid-1970s of the dramatic and serious impact that a liberal trade policy in this area can have. Largely as a result of a government tracking study which monitored the effect of job loss on workers over this period, we also have a fairly good indication of the effects on women. The study examined what happened to workers in the textiles, clothing, and electrical and electronics industries as import competition led to plant closures and dramatic job losses.[35]

The findings are not surprising. They indicate women were hurt much worse than men. Unemployment rates for women during the mid-1970s increased dramatically while those for men remained relatively stable.[36] Among those who lost jobs, women had a harder time. Men found new work much more quickly than women and many more women than men remained out of the labour force altogether (Table 4). As one might expect, these women tended to be the older, married workers who had been in the jobs which required less skill and education and which paid poorly.[37] For those women who eventually did manage to find jobs, the length of time they were unemployed was considerably longer than it was for men: the average differences in length of unemployment between men and women ranged from ten weeks for clothing and electrical workers to fifteen weeks for textile workers.[38]

An Ontario study of the effect of the 1980-82 recession on workers gives a further indication of the unequal impact of unemployment on women. While 62 per cent of the men who lost jobs were able to find new ones, only 38 per cent of the women were able to do so.[39] The discouraging effect this has on women is evident from the fact that while 9 per cent of the men left the labour force, a much greater proportion – 15 per cent – of the women did. Of those who found jobs, for women it was a longer process: while 43 per cent of the men had new jobs within five months, only 22 per cent of the women did.[40]

What is particularly interesting about the Ontario study is that it also looked at the impact of manufacturing losses on wage rates and shifts in the structure of employment by gender. Here too the implications for women were negative. While men on average improved their wages, women's average wage declined: 25 per cent of the men, but 42 per cent of the women reported earning less than they had before they were laid off.[41] The result was a widening of the wage gap between males and females. Before the layoffs women earned 72 per cent of what men earned – the average wage of those women who found employment after the layoffs was 63 per cent of men's.[42] This worsening of women's relative wage may well be a reflection of the greater concentration of women in occupations considered to be female job ghettoes. The Ontario study found that both men and women shifted occupations and tended to move out of manufacturing occupations into other types of work. However, once again, the shift for women was more dramatic. Of the women responding in the study, 56 per cent were working at processing jobs before the plant closures, but only 25 per cent were working at processing when they found new jobs. The corresponding figures for men were 63 per cent and 43 per cent. Women's shift was almost entirely into clerical occupations. The occupational shift for men was less concentrated in a single occupational group as they moved into managerial, professional, sales, service, and construction jobs.[43] The effect, then, of a decline in the level of employment in the manufacturing sector appears to be greater occupational segregation by gender.

Clearly the experience of the past indicates that women in the manufacturing sector have a lot to lose when restructuring as a result of "market forces" occurs. The two main arguments which have been made so far are, first, that women are concentrated in manufacturing

Table 5
Concentration of Female Labour in Manufacturing
Canada, Ontario and Quebec, 1983

Industry	Canada Total Females Employed	Ontario Number	% of Total	Quebec Number	% of Total
Textiles	18,991	8,629	45%	8,428	44%
Clothing	75,997	22,248	29%	43,875	58%
Leather	12,265	7,237	59%	4,570	37%
Electronics & electrical	29,838	20,874	70%	6,203	21%
Food	40,352	15,493	38%	7,178	18%

Source: Statistics Canada. *Manufacturing Industries of Canada: National and Provincial Areas,* 1983. April 1986.

industries which are least able to resist import competition and the least able to expand export markets. The second point has been that it is women within these industries who become worse off when jobs are lost.

Just who these women are needs to be considered. The government's notion is that for workers who are forced out of certain jobs, there will be "adjustment" programs to help them retrain and relocate for jobs in expanding sectors. The primary problem, of course, is retraining and relocation, and for which jobs. The confusion over the nature of expanding sectors is considerable, especially when one considers that the major "adjustment" model the government uses as its guide sees precisely the industries usually considered most vulnerable as Canada's hope for the future. On the other hand the Macdonald Report itself sees only two industries as being sufficiently strong to expand exports into the United States – these are forestry products and urban transit. However, the Macdonald Report does feel that with proper assistance, women will have the opportunity "to leave low-wage, declining sectors of employment for expanding ones."[44] The likelihood of this occurring is extremely small considering both the characteristics of the workers employed in these industries and the nature of women's experience with government adjustment programs in the past.

The vast majority of women workers in the manufacturing sector who will be affected by free trade are located in central Canada (Quebec and Ontario): about 90 per cent of the female workers in textiles, clothing, leather goods, and electronics and electrical products are in these two provinces. A greater proportion of the female clothing workers are located in Quebec, while more female leather and electronics and electrical workers are in Ontario. In general the risk to women in manufacturing is about equal in Ontario and Quebec. The exception to the concentration in manufacturing is the distribution of women in food processing plants. As was noted previously, there is less regional concentration in this industry than for other manufacturing industries (Table 5).

A study prepared for the North South Institute examined the characteristics of women employed in manufacturing industries most susceptible to import competition. It found that workers in these industries tend to be older than average female workers in Canada; they are much more likely to be immigrants and therefore less likely to speak English or French; they are more likely to be married; and they have considerably lower levels of education than the average female worker in Canada.[45] All of these characteristics mean that these workers, the workers most likely to be displaced, are also the least likely candidates to get new jobs.

While the government has indicated that it intends to help dislocated workers in some way through temporary adjustment policies for workers who are suitably "adaptable", if the experience of the past is any guide at all these programs will not benefit the kinds of female workers who will be displaced in manufacturing. Essentially the requirement that workers meet some criterion of adaptability refers to their willingness to relocate and to be retrained. Relocation requirements are particularly hard on women. For married women in families needing two incomes, relocating is a far from simple matter: most families live where employment is available to males simply because males are paid more. The inability of women to relocate will almost certainly have a bearing on their ability to participate in adjustment programs.

Even if they are eligible in this regard, however, the past experience women have had with government training programs has not been good. As was pointed out in a study on free trade done for the Advisory Council on the Status of Women, older and less educated workers have difficulty meeting the qualifications for programs under the national training act.[46] The primary focus of training programs is to retrain for high-skilled, high-demand occupations in the technical and trade areas. Considering that more than half of the women in manufacturing do not have high school diplomas, and a large proportion were not educated in Canada, it is not surprising that women are substantially underrepresented in the programs which would be most likely to lead to employment. Women account for less than 20 per cent of the participants in the National Training Program. In the Critical Trade Skills Training area their representation, at 4 per cent of all participants, is an appalling indication of failure of initiatives to integrate women into non-traditional job training areas.

Labour Costs

Essentially the "adaptive" behaviour to which the proponents of free trade refer are lower wages and inadequate working conditions. Most of the real adapting which will take place will be as a result of the discipline of the market, rather than as a result of planned government policy. In fact, one of the major arguments put forward in favour of free trade is that market forces are able to deal with "rigidities in labour markets," (the economist's euphemism for the fact that labour resists pay cuts). The idea is that if labour would become more flexible in its demands, Canada could be more competitive internationally. Richard Harris, one of the main economic researchers for the Macdonald Commission is quite explicit about this:

> Wage rigidities are the key factor here. If wages would fall in North America, the true forces of comparative advantage, including factor endowment and market structure determinants, would indicate that the plant actually stay right where it is ... If wage costs were in line with those in other countries, there would be no reason to abandon North American locations.[47]

In this context Harris is referring to North America vs. poor countries and the necessity for workers here "to accept wage cuts which would make North America competitive with the NICs or other developing countries".[48] With this kind of thinking (which is, in fact, the heart of the notion of comparative advantage and the great benefits it could provide "in the long-run") the outlook is bleak indeed. Free trade, on a world-wide basis, would mean much lower wages and a poorer standard of living in Canada.

The question that is relevant here, though, is whether free trade with the United States would have a negative impact on wages and working conditions in the industries where women work? The short answer is that it would, since increasing competition forces firms to reduce costs, a factor which invariably has an effect on labour. But there are specific reasons why competition with American firms will have an effect on Canadian workers *even though wages here generally are not higher than in the United States:* this is especially true in the manufacturing industries where female labour is concentrated.

There is frequently confusion over whether or not labour costs are a key factor in Canada's problems with competitiveness. Canadian business leaders, the government, and academic economists tend to argue that they are. Trade unions argue that they are not. It should be a rather straightforward issue – either wage costs are higher here or they are not. But there are different ways of looking at costs. Trade unions, for example, tend to point to the actual wages paid to workers: Canadian workers, on the whole receive less than American workers. In the industries where women's employment is concentrated the wage differences (taking into account different currency values) between the two countries is slight, with Canadian workers generally receiving less than their American counterparts (Table 6). Nevertheless, total wage costs, relative to the amount produced in Canada, are higher than those in the United States and in many industries labour costs altogether assume a higher proportion of total costs than they do in the United States. In order to show the relative significance of labour costs which reflect these problems, economists refer to "unit" labour costs; they compare the labour costs of production for each item produced. So, while the wages Canadian workers receive are not higher than those workers receive in the United States, unit labour costs are considered to be about 30 per cent higher in Canada.[49] This is commonly presented as a reflection of labour productivity; i.e., labour produces less each hour in Canada than it does in the United States. Expressed in this way, the argument can be weighted heavily in favour of business and government. It appears reasonable to assume that if labour is not as productive here as in the United States, it should not be paid as much. This reasoning is further strengthened by studies which show that real wages in Canada [what workers can actually buy with their income] has increased faster than increases in production.[50] This all seems to point to the fact that labour is paid more than it should be.

There are several important issues concealed by reference to labour productivity and unit labour costs. Labour productivity is not simply a result of labour will, or even skill, but is also a result of conditions of work. If the technology labour works with, for example, is not as sophisticated as that elsewhere, labour simply will not be as productive: the level of capital investment is critical in determining the level of labour productivity. Other cost issues are also important. In many industries the relatively small scale of production in Canada cannot allow the economies in production which are possible in the United

Table 6
Average Hourly Wages of Production Workers
In Selected Industries – Canada and U.S.
(in Canadian dollars)

	1981		1982		1983	
	Canada	U.S.	Canada	U.S.	Canada	U.S.
Textiles	7.06	7.07	7.82	7.78	8.31	8.36
Knitting	5.57	6.15	5.99	6.67	6.23	7.00
Clothing	5.76	5.78	6.24	6.21	6.61	6.47
Footwear	5.70	5.78	6.12	6.32	6.36	6.53

Source: *Textile and Clothing Board,Study of the Impact of Potential Free Trade in Textiles and Clothing Between Canada and the United States*, Table 18 (Ottawa, 1984); Canadian Import Tribunal, *Report Respecting the Canadian Footwear Industry* (Ottawa, June 1985), Table XVI.

States. As a result, each item costs more to produce. In some industries the very fact of being located in a large, cold, northern country means that unit costs will be higher. The argument regarding the unnatural growth in wages relative to growth in output in recent years also is not as compelling as it might seem. In many cases the relatively rapid growth in wages is more a reflection of past failure to keep wage settlements in line with productivity growth than with inordinate demands from labour. The main point is that conclusions cannot be drawn about the role of labour costs in placing Canadian industry at a competitive disadvantage simply from data about unit labour costs and relative growth in real wages. These costs cannot be seen in isolation, but must be viewed in the context of the cost structure of the industry and the economic realities of the country. The major problem is that since labour costs have been so strongly identified as one of the major problems for Canadian industry, labour undoubtedly will be squeezed as the pressures of free trade force business to cut costs. This will occur even though workers in Canada are not paid more than workers in the United States.

The manufacturing industries where women work are, for the most part, at a cost disadvantage relative to their American counterparts. The following brief examination of the major industries will give an indication of the responsibility of labour for these higher costs.[51]

In the food and beverages industries costs in Canada are about 27 per cent higher than those in the United States. Material costs account for about 80 per cent of total costs in both countries, but unit material costs in Canada were 34 per cent higher. As was noted earlier, this is largely because of geographical circumstances which make food more costly to produce in Canada. But in some cases higher costs are a result of supply-management schemes. While these schemes are often criticized by processors, they have been designed to protect Canadian food producers and to ensure that Canada will have some measure of self-sufficiency in food production. Unit labour costs traditionally have been higher in Canada, but between 1983 and 84 American costs increased by 38 per cent while Canadian costs remained stable. The result is that in this industry at present Canadian unit labour costs are only 16 per cent above American levels.

The footwear industries have had a distinct cost disadvantage relative to their American competition. However, labour costs are not the root of the problem. While unit labour costs were about 10 per cent above American levels in the early 1980s, in 1984 these costs declined by 10 per cent while American labour costs increased by 42 per cent. This gave Canadian producers a 30 per cent cost advantage in labour costs. Still, Canadian costs greatly exceeded levels in the United States primarily because material costs have been growing in Canada while they have been declining south of the border. American producers have a 61 per cent advantage over Canadian producers in this aspect of costs. Material costs account for 60-65 per cent of total costs in both countries. It is important to note that the protection Canadian industry has received through tariffs and quotas has not resulted in increased wages.[52] According to the tribunal on footwear, Canadian wages are somewhat lower than those in the United States and are, in fact, at realistic levels in an industry where prices are set in world markets. In comparison with other industries, wages in this sector are particularly low. While the average manufacturing wage in Canada in 1983 was about $11 an hour, the average wage in the footwear industry was $6.36 an hour.[53]

Production costs in the textile industries in Canada are generally higher than in the United States. Wages in textiles account for a greater share of total costs in Canada, but wages paid to Canadian textile workers are not higher than those paid to textile workers in the United States. Wages assume a greater share of total costs here essentially because of differences in efficiency as a result of the relative absence of specialization and economies of scale. The costs of most raw materials are also higher in Canada.[54] Overall Canadian costs are about 25 per cent higher than those in the United States. Because of the problems with the size of production runs, unit labour costs have been growing in Canada, while they have been declining in the United States in the past few years.

As a consequence unit labour costs in Canada are more than 100 per cent of those in the United States.

In the clothing industry Canadian producers have had higher total costs than American producers since 1974. However, these costs are primarily due to greater costs for fabrics here than in the United States. The share of labour costs in total costs is less in Canada than in the United States.[55] In the Canadian knitting industry average wages are about 10 per cent less than in the United States. However, Canadian unit labour costs are more than 100 per cent above American costs.

In the production of electrical and electronic products Canadian costs are considerably above those in the United States. Differences in material costs account for most of the cost disadvantage Canadian producers face, but unit labour costs, which are about 16 per cent higher in Canada, are also significant. The drop in labour productivity relative to that in the United States during the 1980s is largely a reflection of the scale of production and the type of product mix produced in Canada.

Despite the general cry from producers that labour costs are too high, in the manufacturing industries where women's labour is concentrated, wages are considerably lower than those paid in other manufacturing industries in Canada. In textiles wages are about 80 per cent of the average wage in manufacturing; in clothing and knitting wages are about 60 per cent ; and in footwear the average wage is just a little more than half of the average.

Effect on Wages and Working Conditions

To date, the discussion of the effect of free trade has been more focussed on what would happen to industries than what will happen to people, but when the impact on labour has been discussed by academic economists or government officials, the effect it will have on levels of employment in various industries has been the main focus. Free trade will require substantial changes, many of which will result in higher levels of unemployment. But the threat to labour will not affect just those who will face unemployment: it is also likely to affect the type of labour legislation which exists in Canada, and the ability of unions to protect the interests of workers.

The American competition in the industries where women are concentrated comes from states with low minimum wages and poor labour legislation. This competition is likely to get stronger as a certain level of production shifts from Canada to the United States. The constant complaint of many Canadian manufacturers whose businesses are threatened by a free trade agreement is that they will be unable to compete because of uncompetitive labour costs in Canada and because of favourable labour legislation which permits workers to have more influence on employment conditions here. In particular they feel the more stringent labour legislation in the United States gives their major competitors a decided advantage and permits them to avoid the kinds of fringe benefits which make the wage bill higher here.[56]

The difference in the Canadian and the American rate of unionization is quite startling. While the Canadian rate, at almost 40 per cent of the labour force, is not high by European standards, it is about twice that of the United States. The differences between the two countries are not because the United States has traditionally followed a different pattern than Canada, but because conditions in the United States make it difficult for unions to survive. The proportion of American workers who were unionized dropped from a level which was roughly similar to that in Canada to one of less than 20 per cent. Most of this drop occurred in the 1980s.[57]

While disaffection with trade unionization is often cited as a major contributing factor to their decline in the United States, the impact of damaging labour legislation is probably even more significant. A major case in point is the existence of right-to-work legislation in many states. About eighteen states have this legislation which, in effect, means that all workers in an establishment do not have to join a union or pay union dues. The effect on the ability of unions to maintain their strength can be devastating. An American study conducted by the National Bureau of Economic Research on the effect of this type of legislation on union organization showed that the impact is dramatic and immediate. The most significant effects occur just after the passage of the legislation, but the consequences continue to be felt even in later years. Generally, a 5-10 per cent reduction in union strength is experienced as a result of the passage of right-to-work laws.[58]

Another legislative problem contributing to union difficulties in the United States is the representation vote the national Labor Relations Board orders every time a union applies for certification. In Canada, a representation vote is only necessary in two jurisdictions: British Columbia and Nova Scotia. Other jurisdictions require the vote only if a certain proportion of the employees have not been signed up. For example, in Ontario if 55 per cent of the workers have joined the union, a vote is generally not taken. The American requirement of a vote for certification makes the organizing work of unions twice as hard as it should be: it sets the stage for a campaign that pits the employer against the union in what often becomes a long battle for the workers' vote immediately after the major effort to organize has been successful. Many unions fail at this stage.

The existence of labour legislation in the United States which employers find more compatible with their objectives is likely to have an effect on labour legislation in the future in Canada. As industries are forced to cut costs to become more competitive they will put considerable pressure on governments to bring labour legislation here more in line with that in the United States. For example, in a brief to the government about the effect of free trade, the Grocery Products Manufacturers of Canada called specifically for change in labour legislation before they would endorse negotiations for trade liberalization. They argue as follows:

> Some product sectors in Canada are at a disadvantage because the comparative U.S. industries are not as unionized. Therefore, some fundamental realignment in legislated benefits programs and labour union organization will be required. As well, Canadian workers' income expectations will have to be substantially lowered.[59]

These kinds of arguments are likely to have more and more weight with governments throughout the country as industries contract and more workers' jobs are threatened.

The need to maintain a competitive edge will also be a compelling argument in employer's attempts to curtail more progressive equal rights legislation. The main objection to introducing equal pay for work of equal value legislation, for example, is that it will be too costly for industry. While these arguments can be resisted on moral grounds, they will maintain their force as industries and provinces are threatened with rising unemployment rates as a result of free trade. In fact, any social measures which are more progressive than those of our trading partner will be seen as unfairly disadvantaging industry here. These arguments will be powerful disincentives for government action on behalf of women and other disadvantaged groups.

Summary

There are no industries which employ substantial numbers of women in the manufacturing sector which are likely to experience significant export growth as a result of free trade. Women are highly concentrated in industries which serve the domestic market, and these industries are most likely to lose portions of the domestic market through free trade with the United States. Certainly some of the women whose jobs in the manufacturing sector are lost will be able to find employment in other industries. However, past experience with trade liberalization has shown that women fare badly when restructuring occurs. The women who work in manufacturing are particularly disadvantaged because a high proportion of them are immigrants and they tend to be older and have less education than the average woman working in Canada. In addition to substantial job loss, the competitive pressures of free trade will seriously affect the conditions of work for those manufacturing jobs which remain.

Part Two

Free Trade in Services: Its Impact on Women's Employment

The issue of international trade in services is beginning to generate a considerable amount of interest, even though it has received little attention in discussions of free trade in Canada. Yet, it is from the service sector that the United States has potentially the most to gain in a free trade agreement, and Canada has the most to lose.

Trade in services has been the fastest growing area of the international market. It is estimated that trade in services grew three times as much as trade in goods since the early 1970s and that it now accounts for one-third of total world trade.[1] For a giant industrialized nation like the United States, negotiating free trade agreements in services is essential to the maintenance of a dominant position in the international trading environment. However, in Canada there has been relatively little concern about the effect of free trade in services, even though there are indications that Canada does not fare particularly well in trade in services and that the existing problems in this area are likely to grow with increased trade liberalization and penetration of the American service sector into the Canadian market. The reality is that Canada and the United States have opposing interests in the service sector, primarily because the United States is a massive service exporting country while Canada is not, nor is it likely to become one.[2]

A discussion of free trade in services is complex for several reasons.

First of all, arriving at a definition of what constitutes a "service" is harder than it looks. The usual distinction between goods and services is that goods are material and tangible and services are immaterial and intangible.[3] Based on this understanding, the economic universe is conceived by economists as consisting of three major categories: the primary sector (agriculture and resource extracting industries); the secondary sector (construction and manufacturing); and the tertiary or services sector, which includes everything else.[4] However, all economic activity does not fall neatly into one group or another. For example, as one economist noted:

> it is difficult to make a sharp distinction between the activities of an auto assembly plant and those of an automobile repair shop, but the former is invariably classified in industry and the latter is usually regarded as a service.[5]

The introduction of information technology in the production process of many firms has dramatically altered their nature and the way they do business. Some firms which have been manufacturing firms, like RCA, have been reclassified as service companies.[6]

Because services cover a wide range of very different activities it is also difficult to generalize about what international trade in services means. Originally international trade in services was confined to activities which supported trade of goods. These services included shipping and other forms of transportation, banking and financial services, insurance, consulting, and administrative services. But increasingly services are being traded in their own right and less in relation to trade in goods. The present list of the types of services traded is long, including such activities as telecommunications, health services, advertising, marketing, management consulting, personal financial services, motion pictures, leasing, accounting, building related services, technology maintenance, educational services, legal services, travel services, tourism, utilities, entertainment, data processing and other computer services, and franchising.[7]

Even more problematic than a definition of service activities is the realization that when we discuss trade in services we are not concerned simply with the effects of importing and exporting them, but also with the more complex issue of the right of foreign firms to be in Canada (the right of establishment) and to receive the same treatment as national firms do (the right of national treatment).[8] The service sector is looked on by some as the true frontier for American investment: the right of American firms to expand investment in services is seen as offering the same kind of function that American investment in the resource and manufacturing sectors historically provided.[9] As international competition makes resource and manufacturing investment opportunities in Canada less lucrative for American firms, the service sector becomes increasingly attractive.

The impact of free trade on services is of particular concern to women because it is in the service sector that the vast expansion in female employment has occurred in this century and it is in the service sector that the largest number of women have the most to lose. In what follows I intend to show why free trade in services will adversely affect women. One result will be increased job losses, as imported services replace domestic ones. But another significant problem, which will result from the demand for the right of establishment and national treatment, will be the amount of control Canada will be able to maintain over the direction of social, economic and political development. This, in turn, will have an effect on both the conditions of work, and the nature of the provision of certain types of services.

I. The Significance of Services

The "Industriocrats" Obscure the Significance of Services

Most governments do not have a sufficient understanding of the significance of the service sector to economic growth to have a coherent trade policy – Canada is one of these countries. In large part the neglect of the service sector in public policy decision making has to do with the distinction which has been made historically between productive and unproductive economic activity. The notion that services are "unproductive," or do not produce value, has a long and distinguished history. Adam Smith, for example, saw services as parasitic activities dependent on the "productive" activities of manufacturing and primary industries.[10] Smith was certainly more enlightened than the physiocrats (who saw productive activity as occurring only in the agricultural sector), and his focus on industrial activity was, therefore, a step forward. But modern economists have tended to be rather rigid in this regard: just as the physiocrats failed to see the productive nature of manufacturing, the "industriocrats" fail to see the productive significance of services. Today services are treated as incidental to genuine growth. They are viewed as the "mature" phase of capitalism which will occur after the development of the resource and manufacturing sectors does the work of building a strong and healthy economy.

Part of the problem of "seeing" services has to do with the focus of economic theory. The notion of counting, productivity, and comparability are all based on the inputs and outputs of things produced for sale. Today the leading indicators of economic performance are almost totally based on the performance of tangibles: inventory levels and commodity price changes tell us about performance in manufacturing, but they tell us nothing about the sector where the largest portion of the labour force is employed. The best example of this is the primary indicator of American economic performance – the Dow Jones average, which all but ignores the service sector. Only recently did it include a financial service firm in its survey of trend-setting companies.[11] However, the increased significance of service industries has certainly been signalled with the introduction by *Fortune* magazine of the Service 100 Directory.[12]

Because of the focus on tangibles, the counting of services which does occur is hopelessly inadequate. On the national level many disparate and uncomparable activities are lumped together so that ultimately what is measured is quite meaningless. On the international level there is a problem of comparing the service activity between countries because of the incompatibility of statistics relating to services. Also, the inclusion of investment income and government transfers in service totals leads to a problem in distinguishing between these activities and the actual movement of services on the international level.

The general invisibility of services means that their significance to economic development is vastly underrated.[13] When a service economy is described, as it often is, as one in which we "take in each other's laundry", its dynamic aspect is concealed and its significance is dismissed;[14] not to mention the sexist implication that doing laundry isn't real productive work. The result is government policy which is biased toward the primary and manufacturing sectors.[15] For example, the Macdonald Report, which uses three large volumes to examine the state of the economy and to make recommendations for restructuring through trade, devotes almost no space to trade in services and did not find it sufficiently significant to commission studies on the issue.[16] This follows from the general concern in advanced industrial countries about the "deindustrialization" of the economy, or the decline of the manufacturing sector's share in the national product.[17] In this respect, the growth of services is seen in a negative way. The thrust of public policy, then, is to shore up the manufacturing and resource sectors under the assumption that service sector growth is an adjunct to growth in these sectors. This assumption is a huge exaggeration which dismisses the significance of the service sector in stimulating growth in the manufacturing and primary sectors.

The Importance of Service Trade to the United States
Recently the United States, more than any other country, has begun to recognize the significance of the service sector to its international trade performance and has pressed for trade liberalization in trade negotiations. The issue of the "deindustrialization" of the American economy, and the loss of American international markets for manufactured goods has created serious concern about the ability of the United States to maintain its economic strength in both domestic and international markets. That there has been a decline in the significance of the manufacturing sector is clear: since the 1950s manufacturing has dropped from accounting for 30 per cent of the GNP to about 20 per cent, and where about one-third of the non-agricultural labour force worked in manufacturing in the 1950s, today only about one-fifth do. In recent years the decline in the manufacturing sector has been more than made up for by the phenomenal growth of the service sector. While about 1.5 million jobs have been lost in manufacturing since 1979, almost 10 million jobs have been created in the service sector.[18]

But the decline in manufacturing, as a result of increased competition from low-wage countries, has created headaches for the United States balance of trade. The most serious problem is the huge manufacturing trade deficit. While this is responsible for the gigantic over-all American trade deficit of about $148 billion, to a great extent the manufacturing trade deficit has been offset by a substantial surplus in services trade.[19] In fact, while merchandise trade ran deficits in ten of the twelve years between 1972 and 1983, services trade produced a surplus in every year. In five of those years, the United States managed to have an overall balance of payments surplus because the services surplus was so large it offset the tremendous merchandise deficit.[20] In 1986 the surplus on the services account is estimated to be $25 billion.[21]

Nevertheless, the trade-off between manufacturing and services exports has encountered some snags. In fact, the service sector's exports have not been sufficient in recent years to offset the void in trade that has been left by manufacturing, hence the alarming growth in the American trade deficit. The United States provides from 20 to 25 per cent of the world's trade in services and is, by far, the major trader in this area.[22] Also, services are among the fastest growing American exports, rising from about 30 per cent of total exports in 1960 to about 40 per cent in 1983.[23] However, as the United States' ability to increase its service trade grows, mainly due to improved technology in communications and transportation, countries which face greater competition in services have begun to institute restrictions to contain the growing American competition.[24] Even poor countries, which in theory should provide a

ready market for the service exports of developed nations, have taken
strong steps to protect their domestic service industries. Contrary to the
pattern which had developed in countries which industrialized earlier,
the service sectors do not emerge in poor countries only after
industrialization has been established. Rather, the service components
of the economy are significant vehicles of growth and often account for a
substantial part of the nation's employment and income. Perhaps even
more important is the recognition by many countries that the
development of indigenous service industries is critical to maintaining
independent political and economic institutions.[25] The "barriers to
trade" which have been instituted by these countries have considerably
inhibited the growth in American service exports.

It is because of the initiatives of the United States that services are
currently on the agenda in international trade negotiations. So far trade
agreements, such as GATT, have focussed on liberalizing trade in
merchandise and have excluded, for the most part, regulation of trade in
services. While a few service sectors have been the subject of debate
within international organizations and some agreement about their
handling has been reached, there has been a tendency for countries with
growing indigenous service industries to resist American efforts for a
more comprehensive agreement.[26]

The United States first raised the issue of including services in a
general agreement in the Tokyo Round of GATT, and it is clearly an item
to be negotiated in the next round. Increasing the export of services has
become a high priority for the United States. The Trade Act of 1974
included services for the first time within the negotiating power of the
president. Now a variety of government agencies have special divisions
to deal with promoting service exports. The Services Industries
Development Program in the Department of Commerce, for example,
has a specific mandate to promote American trade in services.[27] The
Trade and Tariff Act of 1984, considered by many to be a landmark piece
of legislation, grants services full parity with goods under American
trade law and further strengthens exports of services as a priority for the
government. These initiatives have been strongly pushed by the
business community. A powerful coalition of services companies,
including such giant firms as American Express, Price Waterhouse, CBS,
Citibank, American International Group, ARA Services, and The
Interpublic Group of Companies, was formed in 1982 specifically to
build public awareness of the role of service industries in the American
economy and to urge the government to promote the export of
services.[28]

The United States has made considerable efforts to see that services get priority in the next round of GATT. In preparation for the discussion of the service sector, countries have been urged to provide background studies to indicate problem areas and potential solutions.[29] What is clear from the papers which already have been released is that there is no consensus about whether services can be treated within GATT in the same way that merchandise is treated at present. The issues are complex and any changes in existing GATT regulations will take many years of careful negotiating. For this reason, negotiating bilateral arrangements is important to the United States. Bilateral agreements will strengthen the American trading position with individual countries and their bargaining position within GATT. The United States has successfully negotiated a trade deal with Israel which includes services and is now attempting to repeat its success with Canada.

Because of the problems of deciding which services are traded internationally, it is difficult to accurately document the expansion of American service industries internationally. Some analysts estimate that the balance of payments, as currently compiled, underestimates the volume of American services trade by as much as 50 per cent.[30] This has not prevented the American government from recognizing just how important this sector will be for developing a more healthy trade picture in the future and negotiating free trade in services is probably the single most important issue in its deliberations with Canada.

What's At Stake for Canada

Canada's economy is a service economy, yet this is not reflected in our trade figures. Like other industrial countries, Canada increasingly relies on the service sector to generate jobs with services making up a larger and larger portion of the GNP. In these respects Canada's economy is even more service-oriented than those of many other industrial nations.[31] Services account for about two-thirds of the national income and provide about 70 per cent of the jobs in Canada.[32] Of the new jobs created in Canada during the last decade, over 80 per cent have been in the service sector.[33]

While Canada's domestic economy, then, can be described as a service economy, our international trade does not reflect this (Table 7). The peculiar feature of Canada's trade, unlike that of other industrial countries, is that our service account is in deficit. In fact, for the past thirty years there has been a deficit in services, a deficit which is growing at a rapid rate. This is particularly alarming considering that the surplus on the merchandise current account has been reduced drastically, falling steadily from almost $21 billion in 1984 to $17 billion in 1985 and to an estimated $11 billion in 1986. At the same time the services current

Table 7
Canadian Balance of International Payments
Current Account, 1984 And 1985
(millions of dollars)

	1984	1985
Merchandise	20,725	17,476
Non-merchandise services		
travel	-2,126	-2,104
freight and shipping	468	457
business services	-2,181	-2,095
government transactions	-641	-674
other services	96	119
Total services	-4,383	-4,298
Investment income	-13,794	-14,598
Transfers	814	836
Total Non-merchandise balance	-17,364	-18,060
Total Balance of Trade	3,362	-585

Source: Statistics Canada. *Quarterly Estimates of the Canadian Balance of International Payments*, Third Quarter 1986, Table 1. Not seasonally adjusted.

account deficit has increased from $17 billion in 1984 to an estimated $21 billion in 1986. This means that in two years, because of a decrease in the merchandise surplus and an increase in services deficit, Canada's balance of payments on the current account has shifted from a surplus of over $3 billion to a deficit of about $9 billion.[34]

A large portion of Canada's service deficit is due to interest payments to foreign investors and payments by Canadian subsidiaries to their parent firms. As long as foreign ownership of Canadian firms remains at a high level, these aspects of the service deficit are unlikely to change. Although the problem of measuring the service sector's performance is considerable, from the information which is available it can be seen that most of the major service items are in deficit. Aside from the huge deficit in investment income, Canada also has a large deficit in business services and travel. The traded business services which contribute most to the service trade deficit are management and administrative services; royalties, patents and trade marks, films and broadcasting, and equipment rentals. The overwhelming source of the deficit in these areas is with the United States (Table 8).

Table 8
Canada's Balance of Trade in Business Services
with the U.S., EEC, and All Countries, 1984
(millions of dollars)

	U.S.	EEC	Total
Consulting & other professional services	44	14	681
Transportation & related services	-12	-53	-84
Management & adminis- trative services	-748	-8	-752
Research & Development	-221	-10	-238
Commissions	41	60	94
Royalties, patents & trademarks	-846	-48	-934
Films & broadcasting	-113	-26	-142
Advertising & promotion	-26	5	-18
Insurance	-59	-69	-170
Computer services	36	n/a	53
Equipment rentals	-259	-41	-307
Communications	66	-20	42
Tooling & other automotive services	-27	n/a	-12
Other	-192	-56	-231
Total	-2,390	-344	-2,181

Source: Statistics Canada. *Canada's International Trade in Services: 1969 to 1984,* Table 7, June 1986.

Canada's service trade with the United States has deteriorated considerably since the 1970s. The American market now accounts for about 52 per cent of Canada's service exports. This is a drop of about 16 per cent since 1973 when exports to the United States accounted for more than 68 per cent of the total. At the same time the imports of services from the United States have consistently provided about 64 per cent of Canada's service imports.[35]

The problem for Canada is that a deficit in the services account has implications for the level of national employment. As the economy relies more and more on trade with the United States the employment content of what we export will be increasingly reflected in the unemployment rate. Although Canada's is an "extroverted" economy, our trade tends to be centred in industries which are relatively capital intensive and we tend to export items which involve considerably less value added than the items we import.[36] This means that we are importing things which have a greater labour content than those that we export.

Previous moves toward trade liberalization have not brought about increases in Canada's ability to export items with more value added.[37] Considering that the bulk of the labour force is in the service sector, the spectre of job losses in this sector as a result of increased competition from giant American service firms is particularly alarming. At the same time Canada clearly is not likely to be able to bring about dramatic changes in its service exports to the United States; even the pro-free-traders here in Canada do not expect Canada to become a major exporter of services. As the Macdonald Report concedes, there are advantages for the United States in gaining greater access to the Canadian service market. But, it reasons, because of these advantages, the United States would have an incentive to "offer guarantees of improved access for goods exported from Canada."[38] This is peculiar reasoning – at least in terms of what Canada would have to gain. Since a much larger portion of our labour force is engaged in providing services than is engaged in manufacturing, the trade-offs will be extremely lopsided. The real concern for Canada is that there will be considerable erosion of the domestic service economy.

Of course, many firms in the service sector enjoy some kind of "natural" protection and will not be threatened by increased competition. These are firms, such as dry cleaners, hair dressers, printers, auto repair shops, local transportation, and shoe repair, which service small local markets. But as secure as some of these areas seem, there are other areas, most notably in data processing, finance, insurance, advertising, culture, and transportation, where the elimination of protective barriers to trade will create dramatic increases in American competition.

The seriousness of this issue for Canada had been summed up in a statement made by a delegation of the Commission of the European Communities Press and Information Service who studied Canadian services:

> From a Canadian perspective the evidence suggests that Canadian policy makers have very good reason to be concerned about their service trade, specifically their increasing indebtedness, the deterioration in their account with the Americans in most areas and the fragile nature of their service exports growth areas."[39]

The Significance of Service Employment to Women

The vast majority of working women, almost 83 per cent, are employed in the service sector. An even larger proportion are working in service-related occupations. That is, within the manufacturing, agricultural, and resource-extracting industries there are a number of service-related jobs. In all, almost 87 per cent of the jobs women hold in Canada are service-related (Table 9). Any policy, then, which will affect services will have a dramatic impact on women.

The huge increase in women's employment in Canada after World War Two was directly related to the expansion of the service sector of the economy. The industrialization of the economy, with the expansion of the manufacturing sector, brought more women into the labour force at the end of the 19th century, but manufacturing has been of decreasing importance to women in this century so that at present this sector accounts for a relatively small proportion of women's jobs.[40]

The most important changes in the distribution of the female labour force occurred in two distinct periods: between 1911-21 and 1941-51.[41] The 1911-21 period was significant for the dramatic shift in women's employment away from manufacturing. This was a result of economic changes and what has been termed the "Administrative Revolution" in the Canadian office.[42] The proportion of women working in manufacturing decreased from 26 per cent to less than 18 per cent, while the proportion of women working in clerical occupations increased from about 9 per cent to almost 19 per cent.[43] The 1941-51 change was more associated with the dramatic increase in the proportion of women who were working and the fact that more of these women were likely to be married.[44]

The acceleration in growth in the service sector after World War Two, as a result of changes in the structure of the economy, brought married women in large numbers into the labour force. During this period there were also significant changes in the nature of the service jobs women were likely to perform. Service occupations have always been important types of work for women, but as the economy has become more modern, there have been shifts in the type of work women have done in the service sector. The biggest change has been away from personal service (i.e., work as servants, cooks, waitresses, cleaners, hairdressers, babysitters) toward clerical jobs. At the turn of the century 42 per cent of all women working for money were engaged in jobs in personal service and the vast majority of these were domestic workers. Even as late as 1941, over a third of the female labour force was engaged in personal service. But between 1941 and 1951 the most important service-related occupations were related to clerical work. In 1941 over 34 per cent of the

Table 9
Female and Total Employment*
by Major Service Occupational Groups
Canada 1986

Occupation	Total (000)	Female (000)	% of all female workers	% female in occupational group
All occupations	12,870	5,523	100	43
All service-related occupations	8,561	4,798	87	56
Service Categories:				
Managerial, administrative & related occupations	1,454	502	9	34
Natural science, mathematics & engineering	430	72	1	17
Social science & related	204	117	2	57
Religion	35	8	-	23
Teaching & related	535	328	6	61
Medicine & health	595	468	9	79
Artistic, literary, recreation & related	214	90	2	42
Clerical & related	2,096	1,674	30	80
Sales	1,209	530	10	44
Service (personal)	1,789	1,009	18	56

* Labour force 15 years and over

Source: Statistics Canada. *The Labour Force,* Table 65. Dec. 1986.

female labour force was in personal-service jobs, a figure which dropped to 21 per cent in just ten years. At the same time the proportion of women in clerical occupations rose from 18 per cent to almost 28 per cent.[45] These shifts were accentuated in subsequent years, so that by 1981 clerical occupations accounted for over 36 per cent of women's jobs while personal service jobs account for less than 16 per cent. However, in the past five years there has been a rather surprising decrease in the proportion of women holding clerical jobs while there has been an increase in those working at personal service occupations. Now 30 per cent of all working women hold clerical jobs and over 18 per cent have personal-service jobs (Table 9).

Clerical-type jobs are by far the most important ones for women in Canada, at least in terms of the proportion of women employed, and women now account for the vast majority of all clerical workers. In fact, the feminization of these jobs has been one of the major changes to have occurred in this occupational group in this century. At the turn of the century women were only about one-fifth of all clerical workers, by 1961 they accounted for about two-thirds, and today, over 80 per cent. The most significant clerical occupations, in terms of the numbers employed, are those related to typing, bookkeeping, account recording, and data processing. These types of jobs account for about 70 per cent of all female clerical workers.[46]

Personal service and sales occupations are the next most significant occupational categories for women. Within personal service, the most important occupations are those related to food and beverage preparation and service, hairdressing, child care, and cleaning occupations. These occupations account for over 85 per cent of the women working in the personal service category.[47] The most significant sales occupations for women are those as sales clerks. These kinds of jobs account for about two-thirds of all the women working in the sales categories. The other important service-related jobs for women are those in medicine and health fields, and those related to teaching. In medicine and health almost 80 per cent of the jobs are related to nursing. Altogether, the clerical, personal service, sales, teaching, and health related jobs account for almost 85 per cent of the service-type jobs which women hold.

Some types of women's work in the service sector will be unaffected by a free-trade agreement simply because of their very personal and local nature. The jobs most obviously at risk are in the industries where services can increasingly be provided from outside the country. In areas like data processing, telecommunications, transportation, financial services, and culture, there now exist certain types of nontariff barriers to trade which serve to protect some jobs. But the elimination of these protections is not the only issue to be considered. With very rapid changes in technology it is often very difficult to anticipate just what types of services may be provided from without the country in the future. Therefore, the nature of an agreement is extremely important. If it is a general agreement, with specific issues spelled out, industry by industry, we may be unable, at any time in the future, to protect an industry or jobs which are not now protected, but which may need to be as circumstances change.

There are many types of jobs which would appear to be immune from the repercussions of free trade because they relate to services which must be provided within the country. Day care and health services are two such examples. However, there are important issues being negotiated which could affect even these types of jobs. The issues of right of establishment and right of national treatment could mean a restructuring of the way in which certain services are delivered. This, in turn, could affect both the availability of certain services and the conditions of work within service industries. The effect of free trade on services supplied within the country is often not easy to see because the impact will not be direct. In what follows I will discuss the complex variety of factors which are likely to affect both traded services and nontraded services in a free-trade agreement.

II. Issues in Bilateral Free Trade

Delivering Services: Imports versus Investment
Just what constitutes trade in services is not as straightforward as it might seem. Traditionally, trade has been considered to be a transaction between residents and nonresidents. So, when a firm located outside the country sells a service in Canada, it is easy to identify it as trade. But two issues complicate the understanding of what trade in services means. First, in some cases it is extremely difficult to separate service trade from trade in goods because many goods producing industries also include the sale of services. Second, the issue of importing, for many types of services, is of considerably less importance than the right of firms to deliver the service in the host country (the right of establishment). Both of these issues complicate how trade in services can be understood and what trade liberalization of services will mean to jobs and Canadian control of the direction of the economy.

Services are intangible items and some are traded internationally without any direct relationship to things. Such services include activities like banking transactions and insurance sales as well as professional services such as those provided by accountants, architects, lawyers, engineers and information specialists. Other services are integral to the provision of goods and include trade in films, records, books, computer tapes, and repair and maintenance activities which accompany the sale of items like computer hardware. For many services, then, the ease or difficulty with which goods are traded affects the extent to which associated services are traded. As trade is liberalized for goods there may also be notable increases in the trade of services.

The way in which services are delivered raises another issue which complicates the way in which trade in services is handled. It is often difficult to characterize the nature of international service activities – in particular whether they are export or investment-related activities. Most tend to be both, but the distinction between investment and trade is important. The same process can be considered in a different way depending on the way it is provided. For example, when a computer centre located outside the country provides data processing for firms in Canada, the activity is "trade." However, if a similar service is provided locally by an American firm with a subsidiary in Canada, it is an "investment" activity.[48] Yet, whether a service is provided through investment or trade is often a result of the kind of trade policies which exist. For example, many service firms, such as banks, insurance, and advertising firms, could conduct more of their business through trade if regulations (considered to be barriers to trade by foreign firms) did not usually require the establishment of facilities here.

While removing trade barriers which inhibit the importing of services by foreign firms is one goal of bilateral negotiations, it is by no means the most significant one. The real issues for American firms are the right of establishment and the right of national treatment; because obviously, any policies which inhibit their operations here restrict their ability to sell services. Foreign direct investment is much more important and more dynamic to the United States than "trade" in delivering services to foreign markets.[49] For most companies which operate internationally, the distinction between trade and investment is academic. The view generally held is that an international agreement in services cannot be negotiated if it does not include the free mobility of capital. As an IBM executive stated in an address to the Conference Board:

> I strongly contend that the right to establish a local presence is critical in respect of certain kinds of trade in services, particularly those services which relate to the so-called "high-tech" activities.[50]

Existing Barriers to Service Trade

The government, particularly members of Simon Riesman's team, often argue that the concerns about the service sector are largely unfounded since free trade in services already exists to a large extent and negotiating a free-trade agreement would not change current practice in substantial ways.[51] This perspective reflects a particularly narrow view of what constitutes trade in services and overlooks the nature of some of the most potent means of protecting Canada's service sector.

Because services are intangible, tariff barriers generally are not an issue, except in cases where tariffs on equipment make foreign service producers less able to compete in Canadian markets. One example of this is the tariffs on computer hardware. While there has been considerable objection to these tariffs, they have, in fact, been reduced considerably by the Tokyo Round of GATT and are currently at a rate of 4 per cent or less.[52]

However, the nontariff barriers which exist are considerable and provide protection both from the importing of services through "trade," and the provision of services by foreign firms within Canada. What is considered a nontariff barrier is a subject of considerable debate, but it is important to note that there is a tendency for the American government and firms to see a great many activities which are considered normal operations on the part of the Canadian government as serious obstacles to their access to the Canadian market.[53] The following is a brief overview of some of the nontariff barriers to trade in services which have been most criticized by foreign business. They are classified under two major headings: those barriers directly aimed at limiting foreign service industries' activity through control over the level of investment, ownership, and trade; and those less direct, more traditional ways used by the Canadian government to solve the economic and social problems of the country, but interpreted as limiting foreign investment and trade.

Canadian Controls Designed to Regulate Foreign Competition

The major target of American criticism was the Foreign Investment Review Agency (FIRA) until this agency was abolished by the current government soon after it was elected.[54] The purpose of FIRA was to monitor foreign investment and to permit foreign firms to establish or increase activity in Canada only when they would provide a "significant benefit" to the country. In practice the interpretation of what was considered a benefit to the country was extremely lenient and very few applications were denied. What is particularly interesting with regard to the service sector was the relative significance of these applications to overall applications. Between 1974, when FIRA was established, and 1982 about 2,500 applications for foreign investment in the service sector were received; a figure which was considerably more than that for the manufacturing and resource industries combined. While FIRA accepted the vast majority of these applications, there were signs that it was beginning to view applications from American service industries as potentially more harmful to the Canadian economy: between 1980 and 1982 about 15 per cent of the American applications in this sector were disallowed.[55]

With the abolition of FIRA, the most direct control over increased foreign investment in the service sector has been eliminated and, with this, the possibility of protecting the service sector even when foreign investment would be harmful. Nevertheless, there are still other forms of control over investment which are considered to be barriers to trade.

One area which has received considerable attention is the Bank Act where restrictions prohibit foreign banks from receiving full bank status in Canada.[56] American banks complained bitterly over this during the last review of the Bank Act and continue to maintain that it is an unfair barrier to trade.[57] The kinds of restrictions which are considered unfair are such regulations as those which state that foreign banks cannot hold more than 8 per cent of the total banking assets of the country; that at least half of the directors of a foreign bank subsidiary be Canadian citizens resident in Canada; that a 15 per cent tax will be applied on any finances supplied from outside Canada; and that the opening of each branch requires ministerial authority.[58]

Other examples of direct controls over the level of foreign investment include regulations over investment dealers, particularly in Ontario and Quebec, and federal legislation which prevents non-Canadians from acquiring control of a life insurance company which is Canadian owned.[59] There is also legislation regarding the extent of foreign control over book publishing and television and radio broadcasting stations.[60]

Aside from direct control over the level of ownership and investment in Canada, there is an array of other nontariff barriers which are deemed serious obstacles to foreign service firms. Several of these have been the target of considerable criticism in recent years. Of particular note is the Canadian Income Tax Act, which is seen as discriminatory against American magazine publishers. At issue is the provision in the act which permits a company to claim a tax deduction for expenditures on advertising only when the periodical is Canadian owned or is a Canadian edition of a foreign magazine with substantial Canadian content that is edited, type-set, printed, and published in Canada.[61] American publishers claim this is an unfair trade barrier which seriously limits their ability to attract advertising revenues in Canada. The tax law affects American border broadcasters in similar ways. The law will not permit tax deductions for Canadian advertisers using American border stations to reach Canadian audiences.[62]

The inadequate protection Canada gives to "intellectual property rights" is another issue which has received considerable attention recently. Protection of intellectual property takes the form of such things as trade-mark protection, copyrights, prohibitions against theft of technology, and patents. This issue has recently come to a head as a result of the efforts of American pharmaceutical companies who feel they have inadequate patent protection in Canada. They claim that Canada's Patent Act, which allows companies to make generic drugs (copies of patented prescription drugs), seriously infringes on their ability to compete in Canada. The pressure on this country to conform to the desires of multinational corporations on this issue was so great that even before genuine negotiations on free trade began, the government agreed to introduce changes to the Patent Act which would grant multinational firms a monopoly for up to ten years on any new drugs.[63]

The range of nontariff barriers which less directly affect the provision of services by foreign firms is considerable, but they are no less effective in protecting the Canadian service sector. An example is government procurement policy. It has been noted that there is a tendency in Canada for all levels of government to purchase services outside Canada only when they are not available within the country.[64] This, of course, is considered a barrier to trade by American firms. So too are the requirements for work permits and the other various personnel restrictions (such as professional licensing and provincial hiring practices) which prevent foreign firms from freely importing skilled technicians and administrators to work in their subsidiary operations in Canada. As an IBM executive put it, if firms are operating on an international level,

> They must be free to obtain expert help and assistance from wherever it is available. This means they must be able to access this expertise not only remotely through communication networks, but they must be free to bring people into a country to perform these services on the spot and face-to-face with the local customers.[65]

Any Canadian policy which limits the level of investment of American firms in Canada, or any policy which curtails the free mobility of capital and specific forms of labour is likely to be subject to considerable scrutiny during the negotiations on free trade. But even more significantly, should free trade in services be negotiated, these types of actions will be subject to American trade remedy legislation and may be treated as unfair trading practices. The U.S. Trade & Tariff Act of 1984 has clearly linked liberalization of trade in services with direct foreign investment. It specifically calls for policies to encourage expansion of trade in services through bilateral and multilateral agreements which reduce or eliminate barriers to trade in services and to "enhance the free flow of foreign direct investment."[66]

Indirect Barriers to Trade and the Necessity to "Harmonize" Programs

In the past it was fairly easy to determine what constituted a barrier to trade. When the regulation of trade was confined to tangible items, any tariff, quota, or legislative device designed to protect domestic producers from foreign competition was clearly a trade barrier. As these barriers were removed or reduced through international trade regulations, nations have frequently sought less overt ways to protect their industries. This was often done in the guise of health and safety standards or other forms of consumer protection, national security, and political sovereignty. The difficulty, however, is how to determine which government activities are legitimate and which hamper trade. The issue is complicated by two related factors. First, in trade disputes whether an action is *designed* to restrict trade is less significant than if its *effect* is to do so. That is, a government activity can be challenged as a trade barrier even if that was not its purpose. The second related factor is the very different ideas countries may have about what kinds of activities are proper ones for a government to pursue.

The United States tends to assume that its government relations with business, regions, and groups of people are morally correct and that all other countries which are more interventionist in their economies, or which provide help in different ways, are behaving unfairly. American businesses feel, for example, that they are not "playing on a level field" with their Canadian competitors.[67] The president of the United States International Trade Commission has claimed that the public sector in Canada accounts for about 40 per cent of all economic activity, and that "such active involvement in the private sector has few parallels in the United States and consequently has been viewed by certain American companies as an unfair trade practice."[68]

This perspective calls into question virtually the entire spectrum of government programs related to labour, employment, and regional development which are different from those in the United States. The danger for Canada is that while the United States may not directly say "change your tax system, your health care system, your unemployment insurance system, and your regional development schemes," these programs may be forced to change if Canada is to continue to trade with the United States. The pressure to conform will be indirect. It can happen through the mechanism of American trade remedy legislation.

Any company in the United States facing competition from Canadian firms can file a complaint with the United States International Trade Commission if it feels that in some way its major Canadian competitor has been able to sell a product at a lower cost because of some government program or subsidy.[69] So far these challenges have been applied only to the competition American firms receive from Canadian producers of tangible goods selling in the United States. Issues associated with softwood lumber are a good example of how this works. But the result has been that when the ruling has gone against the Canadian firm, duties were placed on the Canadian product. This usually meant that it was impossible for Canadian producers to sell in the United States because their prices would be too high. All kinds of Canadian programs have been challenged in this way: they include federal, local, and regional develoment schemes, the operation of the national railroads, research and development grants, corporate tax policies, unemployment insurance benefits, and subsidies for lumber companies.[70]

Since services have not been regulated by international agreements, there has been no threat to the way services have been provided in the past. But the whole point of including services in trade agreements is so that they would be subject to some sort of trade remedy legislation. How this would apply to competition which is manifest through American service firms operating within Canada is not entirely clear. Certainly the export of Canadian services is not at issue: imposing countervailing duties, as is done in the case of goods, would not be effective. What is at issue is the ability of American firms to operate in Canada in what is considered to be a free market environment. It is entirely likely that some other regulatory mechanism would be established which would provide compensation to American producers, should Canadian programs be found to be trade barriers to service industries. For the United States, the real point of establishing a new disputes mechanism would be to deal with problems arising from trade in services: the American trade remedy legislation which already exists serves their manufacturing interests very well. But for Canadians, any disputes mechanism of this sort will be a powerful incentive to "harmonize" policies and programs so that they will be in line with those in the United States.

The crucial issue is the extent to which Canada can operate effectively with a different approach to the role of government.[71] The vast majority of government programs which can be interpreted as trade barriers were not designed as trade protection, but were initiated to serve some other specific social, cultural or economic goal. Canada has had distinct problems which have required specific government solutions. The market mechanism has not been adequate to provide for the needs of Canadians. In many cases actions which can be considered subsidies to business, and therefore nontariff barriers, were actually economic instruments of development designed to either stabilize the market or to correct structural weaknesses in the economy.[72] The specific problems we face are largely associated with a very large land area, a fierce climate, and a small population. In order to integrate the society, to ensure that certain goods and services are provided (particularly to small and isolated communities), and to see that regional disparities are not too great, government intervention has been necessary.

The different philosophies the United States and Canada have had in the past about the role of government essentially reflects the different problems, goals, and traditions of the country. At issue is the form and degree of government ownership, regional development policies, subsidies to industry, provision of social services, and the regulation of cultural, transportation and communication industries.

In some respects, to say that *all* Canadian programs are in immediate jeopardy is highly alarmist. The restructuring which would be required through free trade will be massive and will therefore require a great deal of time to accomplish. Nevertheless, it is possible to see the impact which free trade would have from the program changes which have already been influenced by American complaints and those which are being planned as a result. For example, boat construction loans and farm mortgage schemes have been targeted by the United States as unfair subsidies. These programs have recently been phased out by the government, which claims that they are no longer needed. The Forget Commission on unemployment insurance has recommended a whole series of drastic changes, including the elimination of extended regional benefits and the coverage to self-employed fishermen, two elements in our current scheme which have been cited as unfair subsidies to trade.[73] The licensing of timber rights on crown lands to lumber companies, at prices which the American industries claim are artificially low, has received considerable attention. The government's imposition of an export tax to assuage American retaliatory action is directly influenced by the power of American trade remedy legislation.

Privatization and deregulation are closely related to free trade and are the logical outcomes of closer trade with the United States. At the moment almost 80 per cent of Canada's trade is with the United States. In the area of transportation there have been long-standing complaints of unfair barriers to trade in Canada. Since deregulation of trucking in the United States, Canadian trucking firms were able to expand their market share in the United States. Yet American firms continue to be excluded by direct regulation from most Canadian markets.[74] The Canadian direct ownership of transportation, both airways and railways, has been challenged by American firms as both a subsidy to other forms of business and as a direct barrier to the operation of U.S. airlines in Canada.[75] With deregulation, privatization, and free trade, there would be considerably greater scope for American firms to operate in Canada. Clearly the initiatives toward privatization and deregulation cannot be seen apart from the move toward greater reliance on free trade and the concomitant need to bring our ways of operating the economy in line with the way things are done in the United States.

At this point two other issues which are related to Canada's regulatory practices and which have been the target of American objections must be mentioned. The first is the requirement that certain forms of data processing, particularly for banks, occur within Canadian borders. The second is the quotas requiring a certain portion of Canadian content in broadcasting. While Canada's position has been that these regulations are essential to protect the confidentiality of individuals (in the case of banking information) and to protect Canadian culture (through broadcast content regulation) these activities are being challenged as unfair barriers to trade and are likely to be the subject of considerable negotiation during trade talks.

In some cases freer trade has already affected the level of employment. In these cases, it will be argued, negotiating free trade in services will prevent protecting these industries in the future and will likely accelerate the accessibility of the Canadian market to American service firms. In other industries the protection which currently exists will be eliminated, resulting in job loss and downward pressures on wages and working conditions.

III. Threatened Service Industries and Women's Employment

The expansion of jobs in the clerical sector and the public service have been very important for the increased participation of women in the labour force. This section will examine the reasons why the quality and quantity of these kinds of jobs will be affected by free trade.

Data Processing and the Data Drain
Information is the most important service to be traded internationally.[76] With the vast advances in technology in recent years, the ability to

transmit information easily and cheaply throughout the world has increased at an extraordinary rate. International information flows occur in a variety of ways and include such diverse activities as broadcasting, satellite transmission, and traded computer services.[77]

One area of particular concern to women's employment in Canada is the trade in computer related services, and most specifically in data processing. In the current bilateral trade negotiations with the United States, this trade is considered by some analysts to be the most important issue for the United States in negotiating free trade in services.[78] The United States leads the world in communications and computer technology and, as a result, is responsible for 80 per cent of worldwide transmission and processing of data.[79] In the face of the move of more countries to place restrictions on the international flow of data, the United States is eager to have present restrictions removed and to prevent new ones from being instituted.[80]

In recent years, the tendency for American firms to penetrate the Canadian data processing market has grown rapidly and the result has been considerable job loss to women in Canada. A recent study conducted by the Canadian Independent Computer Services Association estimated that 180,000 jobs had been lost between 1977 and 1984 as a result of increased importation of computer services.[81] In 1977 about 12 per cent of companies in Canada had data processed in the United States. By 1981 this figure had grown to 21 per cent, and is now estimated to be at about 25 per cent.[82]

The Canadian data processing market is more vulnerable to American competition than that of most countries. This is not simply because of our proximity to the United States and the fact that we have a common language, but also because a large proportion of our industries are American owned. As was recently noted in *Business America,* American data processing firms with international transactions are most involved serving American customers – rather than foreign firms – in other countries.[83] Because of the relatively high American ownership of Canadian business it is not surprising that Canada is their prime market.

There is another factor related to American ownership in Canada which is even more significant to the data drain. This is the tendency for American based multinational firms increasingly to consolidate their management and administrative functions in their head offices in the United States, a process which is made possible by improved transmission of data across borders. An example of the ease with which this can occur with new communication systems is evident in the case of American Motors of Canada. AMC recently announced that through the use of Teleglobe Canada it would be able to improve data communications between their Canadian and American firms to such an extent that "all data processing, including inventory control and scheduling production, will be done in the U.S."[84] In this case the data processing staff in Brampton, Ontario, was reduced from twenty-three to five, with layoffs occurring in data entry and system operator positions.

The ability of American based companies to concentrate administrative functions at their head offices has had a striking effect on employment levels in their Canadian operations. The Canadian Independent Computer Services Association, which represents about sixty Canadian-owned companies, compared the employment levels to total sales of seventy multinational corporations which operate in Canada, but which have their head offices in the United States. They discovered that the employment level per million dollars of sales was considerably lower in Canada than in the United States and attribute the tendency for American parent companies to employ more workers than their Canadian subsidiaries to their ability to concentrate management and clerical procedures in the United States. Table 10 gives examples of the discrepancy between the employment levels of some American parent companies and their Canadian subsidiaries. Taken as a whole, the seventy multinational companies' subsidiaries in Canada employed four workers for every $1 million in sales, while in the United States there were 7.5 workers for every $1 million in sales.[85]

The concern over the "data drain" is not a new issue for Canadians. A Committee appointed by the Minister of Communications in 1978 and headed by J.V. Clyne stressed the problems associated with unrestricted flows of data.[86] In particular it recommended that

> The government should act immediately to regulate transborder data flows to ensure that we do not lose control of information vital to the maintenance of national sovereignty.[87]

The report was concerned about both the implications of the data drain for job loss and for control over privacy and security. It felt the government should require that all data processing related to Canadian business operations be performed in Canada and in particular that client data should not be exported for processing and storage abroad.

A few years earlier, the Minister for Science and Technology, Hugh Faulkner, warned of the problems of transborder data processing:

> It creates the potential of growing dependence, rather than interdependence, the loss of employment opportunities, in addition to the balance of payments problems, the danger of loss of

Table 10
Comparison of Employment Levels per Volume of Sales
Canadian Subsidiaries and U.S. Parent Companies

Parent	Employees/ $1 M sales	Canadian Subsidiary	Employees/ $1M sales
Xerox	8.7	Xerox Canada	5.2
General Motors	6.7	General Motors	2.8
Ford Motor	5.5	Ford Motor	2.9
Borg-Warner	15.9	Borg-Warner	4.5
IBM	6.5	IBM Canada	3.8
Hewlett Packard	10.2	Hewlett Packard	4.3
Burroughs	10.2	Burroughs	7.5
Firestone Tire	10.8	Firestone Cdn.	8.0
General Foods	4.8	General Foods	5.6
H.J. Heinz	8.5	H.J. Heinz	5.9

Source: Canadian Independent Computer Services Association, "Will Data Be Processed in Canada?" October 1985.

legitimate access to vital information, and the danger that industrial and social development will be largely governed by the decisions of interest groups residing in another country.[88]

The whole issue of "data patriation" became evident to the government through enquiries from multinational corporations who were about to institute such programs and wanted to know what restictions existed.[89] No restrictions against these types of data transfers applied then, and none have been instituted since.

As communications systems become even more sophisticated the likelihood of greater amounts of data being processed in the United States is very high. One of the dangers of negotiating an agreement on free trade in services is that it may not be possible, at any time in the future, to institute regulations to protect employment, privacy or security. At the present, Canada is not entirely without laws which regulate transborder data flows, but there is considerable opposition from the United States to those which do exist. For the most part these laws and regulations were instituted to protect privacy and access to data. One of the most contentious is the Bank Act which requires that any bank operating in Canada must have essential records of the bank on Canadian territory. This restriction has affected the ability of

Canadian banks to move data processing activities out of the country. Also, international banks are required to process data in Canada, even if the parent bank has a centralized processing service.[90] Another restriction on the flow of data is related to tax deductions: in some cases business expense deductions for processing data outside the country are not allowed. These kinds of activities have been challenged by American business as restrictive practices.[91] An AT&T executive recently asserted that "free trade negotiations must address the issues of privacy, sovereignty and access to data – issues in which unnecessary restrictions continue to exist."[92]

The expansion of communication links between Canada and the United States has permitted American companies to have relatively easy access to the Canadian market, while Canadian companies have not been able to improve their access to the American market. This is primarily because American firms are able to serve the Canadian market through privately owned American satellite carrier companies, while Canadian corporations have access only through their telephone companies, which have done little to promote these kinds of services.[93] The tendency for data to flow in a north-south, rather than an east-west direction has implications for the cost efficiency of the data processing firms which are located in Canada. As the volume of business which would support east-west networks declines, costs of operating these systems increase. The Canadian Independent Computer Services Association has warned that the result may well mean that for companies to survive they may be forced to relocate in the United States so they can serve Canada.[94]

Free Trade and the Public Sector
The Pressure to "Harmonize": The impact of free trade on jobs in the public sector is a complex issue and as a result has been given little attention in the current debate. When the public sector has been discussed at all it has been in the context of whether or not social services are "on the table" in the free trade negotiations. While the Canadian public has been assured by the government that our social services are not a subject for negotiation, the reaction of the United States' trade negotiator makes the issue less clear.[95] But whether or not social services are "on the table" or not, they are very much on the agenda and will be affected by the outcomes of the negotiations. This can have serious repercussions for women because it has been in the public sector where major advances in women's employment has occurred in recent years.[96]

As was noted earlier in this paper, the pressure to "harmonize" Canadian programs with those in the United States will occur because of the nature of American trade remedy legislation. While negotiators hope to convince the United States that this type of legislation must be given up, the likelihood of achieving this goal is very slim, unless a new subsidies code which strictly defines unfair trade practices is agreed upon. Even Israel, which has one of the most powerful lobbies in Washington, was not able to get exemptions from American trade remedy legislation when it negotiated its bilateral agreement with the United States. It is unlikely that Canada, with less clout in Washington, will be able to pull it off. American negotiators have been quite explicit in their assertion that while new disputes mechanisms may be put into place, the existing trade remedy legislation would still apply. Clayton Yeutter, American trade ambassador, stated this clearly:

> An extremely difficult issue is presented by Canada's perception that our countervailing duty and antidumping laws unfairly harass import competition ... But there is no possible way that the United States can accept subsidized or dumped imports before or after negotiation of a free trade arrangement.[97]

The harmonization of programs themselves may well have a direct impact on the delivery of certain social services and therefore result in a loss of jobs, but the indirect effects may be even more powerful. For example, there is now considerable effort to bring Canadian tax programs in line with those in the United States. The main impetus for this, as has been freely acknowledged, has been the disadvantage Canada will have in attracting business if there are substantial tax advantages in the United States which are not available in Canada.[98] The result of bringing our tax structure more in line with that in the United States may mean reduced revenues for government and unless there is a willingness to increase the federal deficit, there will have to be cuts in spending in the public sector.

There will also be increased pressures from the private sector to limit government spending. The whole objective of free trade is to make business more competitive. As competition intensifies, business will increasingly demand government restraint. Even now there are complaints of the tremendous burden of providing social services and how payments for certain social programs (such as unemployment insurance) disadvantage them in international trade. Undoubtedly there will be continued pressure on government to limit costs in areas where they are escalating rapidly – like health care. We are likely, therefore, to see more privatization of certain aspects of the system, more contracting out and more reliance on part-time, as opposed to full-time, employment.

Health Services: The increased use of contracting out and employment of part-time workers is already happening in hospitals. In attempts to cut costs, various types of hospital jobs are being contracted out. These jobs range from the most menial, like hospital cleaning, to the best paid, hospital administration. Contracting out has a tremendous impact on wages, working conditions, and type of employment [i.e., part-time or full-time]. But it also affects what kinds of control workers can have over the way they perform their work. With the contracting out of hospital administration we are seeing more and more hospitals being run by American management teams.[99] These administrators tend to institute all kinds of management procedures which were designed for health care in the United States. One of the most effective schemes in reducing the cost of nursing has been the introduction of patient classification systems in the hospitals. Nursing costs account for about half of all hospital costs, so there are strong incentives for introducing cost-cutting measures in this area. Patient classification systems identify the amount of nursing time to be allocated to each kind of illness and schedule nursing time in the hospital on a day-by-day basis accordingly. In hospitals where this has been instituted the full-time nursing staff has been cut to supervisory staff while the major portion of nursing positions have been cut to part-time and temporary positions.

If free trade in services is negotiated so that the right of national treatment and the right of establishment are guaranteed, we may well see much more of our health care privatized and being carried out by American health groups. This is most likely to happen in the provision of services which are particularly costly and difficult for hospitals to carry out, such as in the care of the chronically ill and old people.

Privatizing Other Services: It is often pointed out by economists that many services have not been traded internationally because of the existence of regulations which are discriminatory against foreign suppliers. Many services could be provided privately which are now in the public realm. One economist from the United States listed a variety of services which could be traded internationally if free-trade agreements would include extending national treatment to American firms in Canada. These services included fire protection services, postal services, prisons and correctional facilities, urban mass transit, water supply, and day care.[100] The issue of day care, of course, would be of particular importance to women both as providers and consumers of the service. Under free trade it may be possible that public funding of nonprofit day care centres may be seen as discriminatory against private operators, many of whom are part of giant American day care firms.

This could have very significant implications for day care workers in Canada since the private firms tend to have much lower rates of pay than do the nonprofit day care centres. This could also affect the mode of delivery and become a powerful impetus toward the increased privatization of day care. That is, day care centres which are operated for profit may be in a position to claim equal access to public funding as a condition of right of national treatment. There have already been indications that the Ontario and the federal governments support this idea both through direct funding of private day care operators and the introduction of a child care tax credit.

Transportation and Communication: Free trade is also likely to have significant implications for women working in the transportation and communications industries. The harmonization of regulations will affect all kinds of transportation systems, but those of most direct concern to women will be the changes in the airlines industry. Deregulation of the airlines would change Canadian fare structures so that the more heavily travelled routes would be less expensive as a result of competition.

However, as the Ontario government's report on services pointed out, the resulting loss in revenues would mean that it would no longer be possible to continue cross-subsidizing service on routes that are less heavily travelled. The result will mean a decline in the availability of services in many remote areas of the country and job losses for workers servicing them.[101] Another potential source of job loss cited by the Ontario report would result from the ability of American carriers to service major Canadian centres from United States bases as extensions of their routes.

> Our cities could be served by routes that were "spokes" from major airports of "hubs" in the United States. Our airlines could not as readily use Canadian cities as hubs for competition in the U.S. market, because our cities are located at the northern end of continental routes.[102]

This means that flights servicing the Canadian market could originate in the United States, using American workers. All workers in the airline industry would be affected by free trade and deregulation, however women's jobs are most threatened. A recent study of the impact of airline deregulation on women shows that reservation clerks and flight attendants, the majority of whom are women, experience a dispro-portionate loss of jobs as a result of restructuring.[103]

At the moment the communications industry is a highly regulated industry in Canada: foreign ownership of communications services is prohibited and foreign firms are not granted access to the Canadian market. However the CRTC is considering a major change – the deregulation of long-distance telephone service. This, combined with freer access of American firms to the Canadian market, as negotiated through a free trade agreement, could have a major impact on Canadian jobs and the availability of services. The increase in competition for long-distance service will be intense. At the moment Canadian rates for long-distance calls are considerably higher than in the United States. This is because of the balancing of local and long distance rates in this country. As the Ontario report on services showed, if American firms are given access to the Canadian market there would be strong pressures for a large volume of long-distance service between Canadian points to be routed via American carriers. This may mean substantial reductions in long-distance rates, but at the cost of much higher local rates and intense competition for Canadian firms. There is the real possibility that the competition may threaten the financial viability of our system and perhaps lead to the American takeover of domestic services.[104] It would not be technically impossible for all calls in Canada to be serviced from outside the country. The impact on women's jobs, particularly as telephone operators, could be catastrophic.

Summary

The negotiations for bilateral free trade with the United States has proceeded without an investigation of how free trade would affect service industries. The major federal examination of the effects of free trade, the Macdonald Report, commissioned seventy-two background papers, but not one examined the impact of free trade on the service sector. Since free trade discussions have begun the Ontario government has published an extensive investigation of the service sector in that province. It identified at least five industries which would be exposed to increased foreign competition without the prospect of a commensurate increase in sales in the United States. These are banking, culture and broadcasting, investment dealing, telecommunications, and transportation. The report concluded that it was not possible, as a result of an industry-by-industry examination, to see a net benefit in a free-trade agreement regarding the service sector and advised the Ontario government to oppose any free trade approach based on accepting losses in the service sector in exchange for potential gains in other sectors, as the Macdonald Report suggested.

The strength of the service sector is of vital importance to women workers in Canada since the majority of women are employed in this sector. Free trade in services will cause job loss and downward pressures on wages and working conditions in many areas which have traditionally been growth areas for women's employment: data processing, transportation, and public service occupations.

Conclusion

This spring Communications Minister, Flora MacDonald, told women at a Progressive Conservative Party conference that their future in employment was bound to their willingness to take up the challenge of high technology. She said, "I don't want to come along in 20 years' time and hear women saying 'we're disadvantaged.'" According to the Minister, the changes which are occurring now are massive, but since new technology requires brains, not brawn, it presents an opportunity for women to be equal in a way which was not possible in the past. However, there is a problem, as she sees it, and that is with women themselves: most are not aware of the potential in high technology and shy away from the task of learning how to take advantage of new opportunities.[1]

This approach is consistent with the constant theme of government officials and economists who support free trade: we must not fear the future, but have "faith" that things will work out well. We must be cooperative, patient, and willing to be challenged. Those of us who have been concerned about the impact of free trade on the level of employment, working conditions, and the availability of social services are depicted as short-sighted, fanatics who insist on maintaining the status quo. Women in particular are criticized for rejecting free trade. Richard Lipsey, Senior Economic Advisor of the C.D. Howe Institute recently wrote:

It is ironic that women's groups have called for the protection of existing jobs, even those that provide poverty-level wages in industries such as shoes and cheap clothing and that are in head-on competition with those in the LDCs [less developed countries.] One of the objectives of the CAFTA [Canadian-American Free Trade Area] is to replace such poverty-level jobs with higher-wage jobs that go with the up-market niches that these industries can carve out in the United States.[2]

I have tried to show that even if "up-market niches" are expanded in the United States, for Canadian firms, these markets will be small and women will be the major losers in the reorganization of production for export. But, even worse is the real threat to domestic markets which will come with the increased accessibility of American firms to Canadian markets. The idea that high-tech jobs will compensate for the loss of manufacturing and service employment is pure fantasy. No studies of free trade – even those painting the most rosy picture – indicate that Canada can significantly expand exports of high tech products or services to the United States. Flora MacDonald's message to women is full of promise, but it is false. Some women will be able to find jobs in high-tech industries, but not many.

Free trade will require massive changes in Canada. Even supporters of free trade recognize that the "adjustments" will not be painless: with increased competition plants will close, jobs will be lost, and the tax base of communities will be eroded. But these losses are viewed with equanimity, as something which will be temporary and short-term. The government has assured Canadians that they are instituting an adjustment policy so that jobs will not really be lost to workers: people who are sufficiently adaptable will be helped to find the new jobs which will be created. Officials seem to feel that if workers have a car and a full tank of gas, they will be able to restructure their lives to accommodate whatever happens on the market.

Whether Canadians accept the government view or not depends on the strength of their faith – faith in the private market and faith in the government. The government pressed for free trade negotiations without public debate and without a clear idea of what it was going to mean for specific groups of people, regions, or industries. To some economists, like Richard Lipsey of the C.D. Howe Institute, the request for complete knowledge of who would lose jobs, and compensation for those who lose them, is an unreasonable demand which would slow down change and leave the economy in an underdeveloped state.[3] He sees this as a dangerous move and one which has had no precedent in Canadian trade history. This is undoubtably a clue to understanding the chronic economic problems of Canada. The lack of planning and real knowledge of what public policy will mean for people has not resulted in a happy experience for this country.

There are some interest groups which have a great deal to gain from free trade. In each sector of the economy, and in every industry employers are divided on the issue. Those with the most to gain are the large international corporations who want to be free to locate production wherever circumstances are most favourable, but at the same time want to have complete access to the Canadian market. Those with the most to lose are the producers who can expect increased competition for their share of the domestic market. But whether employers are better off or not, workers, in both cases, lose. A "successful" outcome of free-trade negotiations will not mean the same thing for ordinary people as it does for the rich and powerful.

According to those in favour of free trade a successful agreement would be one which would give Canadian producers greater access to the American market and which would remove barriers to trade on both sides of the border so that production would become more rational. There are two serious flaws to this approach. The first relates to the nature of the trade agreement. When it was first proposed, those of us who recognized its dangers argued that the strength of American trade remedy legislation would mean that any agreement which could be negotiated would have a very different affect for Canada than for the United States.[4] American firms could gain better access to the Canadian market, but unless there were substantial changes in Canadian social and economic programs, there would be little increase in access to the American market for Canadian firms. Being right on this issue is cold comfort now, but even pro-free traders have finally come around to recognizing that the suspension of American trade remedy legislation is the critical issue for Canada in the negotiations. According to Richard Lipsey:

> The present American view would appear to be that countervailing duties should be used to remove international differences in social and economic policies, resource management schemes, environmental control and just about every way in which national differences manifest themselves in differences in broad based policies. Canadians – and rightly so in my opinion – see the current American approach as a direct attack on their sovereignty.[5]

Since the beginning of discussions on free trade, the United States has made it absolutely clear that they will not give in to Canadian pressure to limit the power of their trade remedy legislation. The American government has been consistent and adamant about this issue because they have absolutely nothing to gain by changing their present policy. The sad fact for Canada is that the whole "success" of a free-trade agreement is dependent on changing the American position on this issue. If the United States does agree to a dispute mechanism which limits the power of their trade remedy legislation, it will only be because Canada has acquiesced to a subsidies code which makes the American trade remedy legislation unnecessary.

The second major flaw with the government's reasoning on free trade relates to its understanding of what "success" means. Success cannot be seen merely in terms of whether or not Canadian producers will gain improved access to the United States market. Even if they can obtain this (which I have argued is highly doubtful), trade-led growth is not an adequate economic policy to solve our economic problems. What is missing is a setting of priorities. A free-trade policy is primarily concerned with means rather than ends: it is totally bound up with a *belief* in the "magic of the market." The real problem is that the goals and priorities of people of the country have received little consideration. When the Macdonald Commission toured the country they were told again and again that the major issue for people was unemployment. But the policies the Commission chose to advocate and which the government has taken up, have ignored this issue. Once we embark on the free-trade route our ability to establish priorities, other than those dictated by the private market mechanism, will be relinquished. Trade is important for Canada. We are a great trading nation and will continue to be one. But the main issue now is the role of trade policy: it should serve economic and social goals – not determine them.

Notes

Introduction

1 Lane Kirkland, "Free Trade and Economic Crisis," *The Bulletin of the Department of International Affairs, AFL-CIO,* October 1986.
2 Adam Smith, *The Wealth of Nations* (New York: Random House, 1937), p. 432.
3 Harriet Martineau, *Retrospect of Western Travel* (London: Saunders and Otles, 1838), Vol. I, p. 142.
4 Harris, R.G. with D. Cox, *Trade, Industrial Policy and Canadian Manufacturing* (Toronto: Ontario Economic Council, 1983); A. R. Moroz and Gregory J. Meridith, *Economic Effects of Trade Liberalization with the U.S.A.; Evidence and Questions* (Ottawa: Institute for Research on Public Policy, Sept. 1985).
5 Harry L. Freeman, Executive Vice President, American Express, "U.S.-Canada Free Trade Negotiations: The Importance of Services," paper presented to The Brooking Institution and The Institute for Research on Public Policy Conference on Building a Canadian-American Free Trade Area, Feb. 1987.

Part One

1 *Report of the Royal Commission on the Economic Union and Development Prospects for Canada,* Vol. I (Ottawa: 1985), p. 345.
2 David Cox and Richard Harris, "A Quantitative Assessment of the Economic Impact on Canada on Sectoral Free Trade with the U.S.," *Canadian Journal of Economics* 3 August 1986, pp. 377-394.

3 Textile and Clothing Board, *Study of the Impact of Potential Free Trade in Textiles and Clothing Between Canada and the United States* (Ottawa, 1984), p. 12.
4 Canadian Textiles Institute, "Submission of T.M. Burns, Special Coordinator for Market Access Consultations," August 1985, Table 5. Canada spends over $92 per capita a year on imported textiles and clothing. This compares with $54 in the U.S, $51 in the U.K., $35 in France, $21 in Italy, $22 in Japan. Only Sweden spends more – $176.
5 Ibid., p. 10-12.
6 For discussions of the development and complexities of MFA see Bhagirath L. Das, "The GATT Multi-Fibre Arrangement," *Journal of World Trade Law*, 17, 2 (March-April 1983); The North South Institute, *The Multi-Fibre Arrangement: Unravelling the Costs* (Ottawa, 1985).
7 Michael M. Hart, *Canadian Economic Development and the International Trading System: Constraints and Opportunities*, Vol. 31 *Royal Commission on the Economic Union and Development Prospects for Canada* (Ottawa, 1985), p. 115.
8 Ibid., p. 132.
9 Textile and Clothing Board, *Study of the Impact of Potential Free Trade in Textiles and Clothing Between Canada and the United States* (Ottawa, August 1984), p. 26.
10 Ibid., p. 66.
11 Canadian Textile Institute, Submission to Burns, p. 20.
12 Textile and Clothing Board, *Study of the Impact of Free Trade*, p. 59.
13 "Freer Trade Deemed Threat to Stanfield," *Globe and Mail* Dec. 5, 1986.
14 Canadian Textiles Institute, "Submission to the Special Joint Committee on Canada's International Relations re Bilateral Trade with the United States," (Ottawa, July 1985).
15 Gilbert R. Winham. *Canada-U.S. Sectoral Trade Study*, Unpublished background paper for the Royal Commission on the Economic Union and Development Prospects for Canada (Ottawa, April 1985) p. 34.
16 The Canadian Food Processors Association, "Presentation to the Ministry of International Trade on Bilateral Trade Relations with the United States of America," (no date); Grocery Products Manufacturers of Canada, "Impact Assessment of Trade Liberalization with the U.S." (Toronto, August 1985); Canadian Meat Council, "Comments on Canada's International Meat Trade and Free Trade with the U.S.A.," (Toronto, June 1985).
17 "Impact Assessment of Trade Liberalization with the U.S."
18 The Canadian Food Processors Association, "Presentation to the Ministry of International Trade."
19 Deloitte Haskins and Sells Associates, *Canadian Agricultural Trade Issues*, Vol. I, *Free Trade with the U.S.A.* (Toronto, July 1985).
20 Winham, *Canada-U.S. Sectoral Trade Study*; Canadian Meat Council, "Comments on Canada's International Meat Trade."

21 The Canadian Food Processors Association, "Presentation to the Ministry of International Trade."
22 Winham, *Canada-U.S. Sectoral Trade Study*, p. 228.
23 Electrical and Electronic Manufacturers Association of Canada, Letter to James Kelleher, May 8, 1985.
24 Winham, *Canada-U.S. Sectoral Trade Study*, p. 230.
25 Ibid., pp. 240-41.
26 United Electrical, Radio and Machine Workers of Canada, Presentation to the Select Committee on Economic Affairs, August 26, 1985.
27 Winham, *Canada-U.S. Sectoral Trade Study*, p. 258.
28 Canadian Import Tribunal, *Report Respecting the Canadian Footwear Industry* (Ottawa, June 1985), p. 17.
29 "Plea to renew shoe quotas is rejected in Ottawa talks," *Globe and Mail*, Feb. 13, 1987.
30 Statistics Canada, Cats. 65-007, 65-203; Import Tribunal, *Report on Footwear*, Appendix Table B-13.
31 Ibid., p. 79.
32 Baltimore *Sun*, August 11, 1985.
33 Winham, *Canada-U.S. Sectoral Trade Study*, p. 116.
34 *Canadian Dimension*, 19, 4 (Sept./Oct. 1985).
35 Canada. Department of Industry, Trade and Commerce, *A Report on the Labour Force Tracking Project/Costs of Labour Adjustment Study* (Ottawa, March 1979).
36 Pat Armstrong, Hugh Armstrong, *The Double Ghetto*, rev. ed. (Toronto: McClelland and Stewart, 1984), Table 10.
37 Tacking Study, pp. 14-17.
38 Ibid., Table 8.
39 Ontario, Ministry of Labour, *Labour Market Experiences of Workers in Plant Closures: A Survey of 21 Cases* (Toronto, May 1984), Table V_1.
40 Ibid., Table VII_2.
41 Ibid., Table VI_3.
42 Ibid., p. 27.
43 Ibid., Table VI_2.
44 Royal Commission on the Economic Union, Vol. II, p. 629.
45 North-South Institute, *Women in Industry: North-South Connections* (Ottawa, 1984), chapter 4.
46 Barbara Cameron and Ann Porter, *Free Trade and the Implications for Women (Ottawa: The Advisory Council on the Status of Women, forthcoming.)*
47 Richard Harris, *Trade, Industrial Policy and International Competition* (Toronto: University of Toronto Press, 1985), p. 132; see also D.J. Daly and D.C. MacCharles, "Persisting Unemployment in Canada – New Evidence on an Old Theory," unpublished paper prepared for The Fraser Institute, June 1985.

48 Harris, *Trade, Industrial Policy and Internatinal Competition,* p. 132.

49 Donald J. Daly, "Micro Economic Performance: Interrelations between Trade and Industrial Policies," unpublished paper prepared for the Ontario Economic Council Conference, Canadian Trade at a Crossroads: Options for New International Agreements, April 1985.

50 Donald J. Daly, "Canadian Manufacturing and International Competition," paper presented at the Executive Management Forum, Toronto, November 1985.

51 Unless otherwise stated the cost information discussed in this section comes from a study prepared by Data Resources of Canada, *Unit Cost Comparisons for Canadian and American Industries* (Ottawa: Department of External Affairs, Jan. 1986.)

52 Footwear Tribunal, p. 14.

53 Ibid., Table XV, p. 81.

54 Textile and Clothing Board, *Study on Impact of Free Trade,* p. 44.

55 Ibid., p. 52.

56 Canada Meat Council, "Canada's International Meat Trade;" Grocery Products Manufacturers of Canada, "Impact Assessment of Trade Liberalization with the U.S."; Canadian Food Processors Association, "Bilateral Trade Relations with the U.S.".

57 Keith Atkinson, "U.S. Labor Seeks Some New Teeth," *The Globe and Mail,* August 1, 1986, p. A7.

58 David Elwood, Glenn Fine, *The Impact of Right-To-Work Laws on Union Organization,* Working Paper No. 1116 (Cambridge, Mass: National Bureau of Economic Research, 1983.)

59 Grocery Products Manufacturers of Canada, "Impact Assessment of Trade Liberalization with the U.S.".

Part Two

1 Andrew R. Moroz, "Trading New Services", *Policy Options,* 4, 2 (March/April, 1983) p. 46.

2 U.S. service exports are almost half as large as goods exports, while Canadian service exports are only 15 per cent of goods exports. Frederick F. Clairmonte and John H. Cavanagh, *Transnational Corporations and Services: The Final Frontier,* (United Nations: UNCTAD, 1984) Table 8, p. 230.

3 Russell Lewis, *The New Service Society* (Longon: Longman, 1973), p. 1.

4 Thomas M. Stanback, Jr., Peter J. Bearse, Thierry J. Noyelle, Robert A. Karasek, *Services/The New Economy* (Totowa, N.J.: Allanheld, Osmun & Co., 1981), p. 12.

5 Victor Fuchs, *The Service Economy* (New York: Columbia University, 1968), p. 15.

6 Geza Feketekuty and Kathryn Hauser, "The Impact of Information Technology on Trade in Services", Feb. 1985, unpublished paper.

7 For a general discussion of what constitutes trade in services see William Diebold, Jr., and Helena Stalson, "Negotiating Issues in International Services Transactions", in *Trade Policy in the 1980s,* ed. by William R. Cline (Washington, D.C.: Institute for International Economics, 1983), pp. 581-609.

8 Canada, Task Force on Trade in Services, *Background Report* (Ottawa, October 1982), pp. 65-66.

9 Clairmonte and Cavanagh, *Transnational Corporations and Services: The Final Frontier.*

10 Adam Smith, *The Wealth of Nations* (New York: Modern Library, 1937 (orig. 1776), pp. 315-32.

11 Ronald Kent Shelp, *Beyond Industrialization: Ascendancy of the Global Service Economy* (New York: Praeger, 1981), p. 5.

12 *Fortune,* 107,12 (June 13, 1983).

13 See Clairmonte and Cavanagh, *Transnational Corporations and Services,* for a discussion of growth in services as the dynamic aspect of post-war economies of most developed market economies.

14 Ronald K. Shelp, "The Service Economy Gets No Respect", *Across the Board: Conference Board Magazine,* XXI, 2 (February 1984), p. 50.

15 Shelp. *Beyond Industrialization,* p. 76-77.

16 Report of the Royal Commission on the Economic Union and Development Prospects for Canada (Ottawa: 1985).

17 This is a dominant theme in both the United States and Canada. The March 3, 1986 issue of *Business Week* ran several articles on the topic. The titles were "The Hollow Corporation: The decline of manufacturing threatens the entire U.S. economy", "Even American Knowhow is Headed Abroad: Deindustrialization is robbing the U.S. of more than just blue-collar jobs"; "And Now, the Post-Industrial Corporation". See also, James Laxer, *Leap of Faith* (Edmonton: Hurtig, 1986); Abraham Rotstein, *Rebuilding from Within* (Ottawa: Canadian Institute for Economic Policy, 1984); Cy Gonick, *Out of Work* (Toronto: Lorimer, 1978).

18 "The Hollow Corporation", p. 59.

19 $175 billion is estimated to be the American trade deficit for 1986.

20 Stanley Ginsberg and Robert Hamrin, *Services the New Economy* (Washington: Coalition of Service Industries, 1985.)

21 Hyman Solomon, "Services Now Issue in Trade Talks", *Financial Post,* Oct. 4, 1986.

22 Joan Edelman Spero, *The Politics of International Economic Relations,* third edition (New York: St. Martin's, 1985), p. 100; Donald V. Ernshaw, "Services", *Business America,* April 30, 1984, p. 10.

23 Ginsberg and Hamrin, *Services the New Economy.*

24 Garth Hewitt, "Now the Invisibles Run into Barriers", *International Management,* 38, 3 (March 1983).

25 Shelp, *Beyond Industrialization,* pp. 77-81.

26 For a discussion of areas where liberalization of trade in services has occurred, see Murray Gibbs, "Continuing the International Debate on Services", *Journal of World Trade Law*, 19, 3 (May-June 1985), pp. 199-218.

27 *Business America*, November 1985.

28 The Coalition of Service Industries is located at 1333 New Hampshire Ave, N.W., Suite 400, Washington, D.C., 20036.

29 Shailendra J. Anjaria, Naheed Kirmani, and Arne B. Petersen, *Trade Policy Issues and Developments*, Occasional Paper No. 38 (Washington, D.C.: International Monetary Fund, July 1985).

30 Kelly, *Business America* March 4, 1985.

31 Task Force on Trade in Services, *Background Report*, (Ottawa: October 1982), Table One, p. 10.

32 *Report, Royal Commission on the Economic Union and Development Prospects for Canada*, (Ottawa: 1985), Vol. I, Tables 2-11, 2-12., pp. 142-143.

33 Task Force on Trade in Services, p. 11.

34 *Globe and Mail*, October 4, 1986; February 11, 1987.

35 E.C. Commercial Counsellors in Canada, *Trade in Services: E.C./Canada* (Ottawa, Dec. 1982), p. 16.

36 Canada has an unusually high proportion of its GNP devoted to trade. In fact, about 80 per cent of all of our trade, accounting for almost a third of our GNP, is devoted to trade with the United States. This is a much greater proportion of GNP devoted to trade with one country than is typical of other industrial countries. For example, for France, Germany, and Japan, trade with their largest trading partner accounts for about 6 per cent of their respective GNPs. (OECD, Monthly Statistics of Foreign Trade (May 1985); and OECD *National Accounts, 1960-1983* (Paris, 1984)).

37 Bruce W. Wilkinson, "Canada-U.S. Free Trade and Some Options", *Canadian Public Policy*, VII (1982), p. 431.

38 *Royal Commission on the Economic Union and Development Prospects for Canada*, Vol. I, p. 309.

39 E.C. *Trade in Services*, p. 37.

40 1961 Census of Canada, Bulletin 3.1-1, Table 3; *Women in the Labour Force 1985-86 Edition* Table I-6.

41 Noah Meltz, "The Female Worker: Occupational Trends in Canada," in *Changing Patterns in Women's Employment* (Ottawa: Women's Bureau, Canadian Department of Labour, 1966), p. 39.

42 Graham S. Lowe, "The Administrative Revolution in the Canadian Office: An Overview", in *Essays in Canadian Business History*, ed. by Tom Traves (Toronto: McClelland and Stewart, 1984), pp. 114-133.

43 Department of Labour, *Women at Work in Canada* (Ottawa, 1963), Table 12, p. 28.

44 For overviews of changes in women's labour in the 20th century see Pat Armstrong and Hugh Armstrong, *The Double Ghetto* rev. ed., (Toronto:

McClelland and Stewart, 1984); Paul Phillips and Erin Phillips, *Women and Work* (Toronto: James Lorimer, 1983); S.J. Wilson, *Women, The Family, and the Economy* (Toronto: McGraw-Hill Ryerson, 1982).

45 *Women at Work in Canada*, Table 12, p. 28.

46 Calculated from Census 1981, Table 2.

47 Ibid.

48 Anjaria, Kirmani, and Petersen, *Trade Policy Issues and Developments*, p. 34.

49 Gibbs, "Continuing the International Debate on Services", p. 210.

50 Grant G. Murray, "Trade in Services from a Business Perspective", Address to the Conference Board of Canada, February 18, 1986.

51 Personal communication.

52 Policy and Strategy Branch, Ministry of State for Science and Technology, *Canadian Trade in High-Technology: An Analysis of Issues and Prospects* (Ottawa, August 1985), p. 16.; de C. Grey, *Traded Computer Services*, p. 13.

53 See, for example, Michael Cohen and Thomas Morante, "Elimination of Nontariff Barriers to Trade in Services: Recommendations for Future Negotiations", *Law and Policy in International Business*, 13, 2 (November 1981).

54 For examples of American criticism of FIRA, see Earl H. Fry, "Sectoral free trade", *International Perspectives (Sept/Oct. 1984)*

55 E.C. *Trade in Services*, pp. 28-30.

56 U.S. Department of Commerce International Trade Administration, *Current Development in U.S. International Service Industries* (Washington: March 1980), p. 39.

57 Kenneth J. Friedman, "The 1980 Canadian Banks and Banking Law Revisions Act: Competitive Stimulus or Protectionist Barrier?", *Law and Policy in International Business* 13, 3 (1981), pp. 783-810.

58 For a full description of Canadian restrictions on foreign banks see, OECD, *International Trade in Services: Banking, Identification and Analysis of Obstacles* (Paris: OECD, 1984).

59 E.C. *Trade in Services*, p. 32.

60 For different perspectives on government restrictions on foreign investment in cultural areas see Steven Globerman, *Cultural Regulation in Canada* (Ottawa: The Institute for Research on Public Policy, 1983); Canada, Consultative Committee on the Implications of Telecommunications for Canadian Sovereignty, *Telecommunications and Canada* (Ottawa: 1979).

61 E.C. *Trade in Services*, p. 31.

62 U.S. Department of Commerce, *Current Development in U.S. International Service Industries*, pp. 30-31.

63 For an excellent analysis of the politics of the generic drug issue see John Sawatsky, "Inside Dope", *This Magazine*, 20,3 (August-September 1986).

64 E.C. *Trade in Services*, p. 30.

65 Murray, "Trade in Services from a Business Perspective".

66 Gibbs, "Continuing the International Debate on Services", p. 212.
67 See, for example, the complaints by U.S. architectural, engineering and construction industries cited by John Austin, "Leaders from Services Sector Voice Trade Concerns to PEC", *Business America*, 6, 14 (July 11, 1983).
68 *Toronto Star* March 17, 1986.
69 Rodney de C. Grey, *United States Trade Policy Legislation: A Canadian View* (Ottawa: Institute for Research on Public Policy, 1982).
70 Peter O. Suchman, "The Impact of U.S. Federal Laws on Sectoral Integration", *Canada-United States Law Journal*, 10 (1985), p. 150.
71 For an analysis of the political problems involved in free trade and the effect this would have on restructuring federal/provincial relations see Marjorie Cohen and Daniel Drache, "Politics: The Heart of the Free Trade Debate", in *Un marché, deux sociétés?*, 1ère partie, *Libre-échange et autonomie politique*, eds.: Christian Deblock et Maurice Couture (Montreal: L'ACFAS, 1987), pp. 187-206.
72 Ibid.
73 Commission of Inquiry on Unemployment Insurance, *Report (Ottawa, November 1986)*.
74 Fred Thompson, "Reducing Barriers to Trade in Nontraded Goods and Services", *Canada-United States Law Journal*, 10 (1985), p. 40
75 Suchman, "Impact of U.S. Federal Laws on Sectoral Integration"; U.S. Department of Commerce, *Current Developments in U.S. Inernational Service Industries*, p. 128.
76 Rodney de C. Grey, *Traded Computer Services: An Analysis of a Proposal for Canada/U.S.A. Agreement* (Royal Bank).
77 For a comprehensive view of the nature and problems involved in international information flows see Hamid Mowlana, *International Flow of Information: A Global Report and Analysis*, Report No. 99 (New York: UNESCO, 1985).
78 de C. Grey, *Traded Computer Services*, p. 2.
79 Hamid Mowlana, p. 45.
80 G. Russell Pipe, "International Information Policy: Evolution of Transborder Data Flow Issues", *Telematics and Informatics*, 1. 4, (1984), pp. 409-418.)
81 W.H. Loewen, "Will Canadian Data Be Processed in Canada?" (unpublished paper prepared for the Canadian Independent Computer Services Association, Winnipeg, October 1985).
82 Cheryl Anderson, Canadian Independent Computer Services Association, address to Council of Canadians, May 15, 1985, Toronto.
83 Mary C. Inoussa, "Data Processing Services: Managing the Information Explosion", *Business America*, May 13, 1985.
84 Martin Slofstra, "AMC plans parent satellite link-up", *Computing Canada*, October 3, 1985, p. 3.
85 "Free flow of data said to have cost 300,000 jobs", *Toronto Star*, April 20, 1986.

86 *Consultative Committee on the Implications of Telecommunications for Canadian Sovereignty*, (Ottawa: Communications Ministry, 1979).
87 Ibid., p. 64.
88 John M. Eger, "Emerging Restrictions on Transnational Data Flows: Privacy Protection or Non-Tariff Trade Barriers?" *Law and Policy in International Business* 10, 4 (1978), p. 1078-79
89 Heather Menzies, "Data exports: a terminal illness?" *Canadian Business* 54, 6 (June 1981), p. 122.
90 Pipe, p. 416.
91 de C. Gray, Royal Bank, p. 7.
92 "Free up data flow across our border U.S. expert urges", *Toronto Star*, October 30, 1985.
93 Lowen, p. 5; George Radwanski, *Ontario Study of the Service Sector* (Ministry of Treasury and Economics, December 1986), pp. 80-82;
94 Lowen, p. 3.
95 Bob Hepburn, "Social Programs, Auto Pact on Trade Block, U.S. Insists", *Toronto Star*, June 19, 1986.
96 *Globe and Mail*, Dec. 18, 1986.
97 Clayton Yeutter, Address to the *Chicago Sun Times* Forum, October 30, 1986.
98 Cathryn Motherwell, "Extent of Tax Reform Still Unclear", *Globe and Mail*, Sept. 16, 1986; Jennifer Lewington, "Canada Pressing Ahead on Tax Reform, Wilson Tells U.S.", *Globe and Mail*, Sept. 6, 1986; Gordon Riehl, "Tax Law Overhaul Will Have to be Brisk", *Globe and Mail*, Sept. 1, 1986.
99 Randy Sykes, "Privatizing Services", *The Facts* 7, 2 (March-April 1985), pp. 36-38.
100 Fred Thompson, "Reducing Barriers to Trade in Nontraded Goods and Services", *Canada-United States Law Journal*, 10 (1985), p. 45.
101 George Radwanski, *Ontario Study of the Service Sector* (Dec. 1986), p. 84.
102 Ibid., pp. 84-85.
103 Joan Hannant, "The Impact of Privatization on Women in Canada", (Toronto: The National Action Committee on the Status of Women, March 1986.)
104 Radwansky, *Ontario Study of the Service Sector*, p. 82.

Conclusion

1 "Brains, not brawn required, minister says," *Globe and Mail*, March 30, 1987.
2 Richard Lipsey, "The Economics of Canadian-American Free Trade Association," in *The Future on the Table: A Critical Analysis of Canada-U.S. Free Trade Issue*, ed. by Michael Henderson, forthcoming.
3 Ibid.
4 Cohen and Drache, "Politics: The Heart of the Free Trade Debate".
5 Lipsey, "The Economics of Canadian-American Free Trade Association".

Selected Bibliography

Anjaria, Shailendra J., Naheed Kirmani, and Arne B. Petersen. *Trade Policy Issues and Developments*. Occasional Paper No. 38 Washington D.C.: International Monetary Fund, July 1985.

Cameron, Duncan, ed. *The Free Trade Papers.* Toronto: Lorimer, 1986.

Canada. Consultative Committee on the Implications of Telecommunications for Canadian Sovereignty, *Telecommunications and Canada.* Ottawa: 1979.

Canada. Data Resources of Canada. *Unit Cost Comparisons for Canadian and American Industries.* Ottawa: Department of External Affairs, January 1986.

Canada. Department of Industry, Trade and Commerce. *A Report on the Labour Force Tracking Project/Costs of Labour Adjustment Study.* Ottawa: March 1979.

Canada. Labour Canada, *Women in the Labour Force 1985-86 Edition.*

Canada. Department of Labour. *Women at Work in Canada.* Ottawa: 1963.

Canada. The Canadian Import Tribunal. *Report Respecting the Canadian Footwear Industry.* Ottawa: June 1985.

Canada. Policy and Strategy Branch, Ministry of State for Science and Technology. *Canadian Trade in High-Technology: An Analysis of Issues and Prospects.* Ottawa: August 1985.

Canada. *Report on the Royal Commission on the Economic Union and Development Prospects for Canada.* Ottawa: 1985.

Canada. Statistics Canada. *The Labour Force.* December 1986.

Canada. Statistics Canada. *Manufacturing Industries of Canada: National and Provincial Areas* 1983. April 1986.

Canada. Statistics Canada. *Summary of Canadian International Trade,* December 1985, November 1986.

Canada. Task Force on Trade in Services. *Background Report* Ottawa: 1982.

Canada. Textile and Clothing Board. *Study of the Impact of Potential Free Trade in Textiles and Clothing Between Canada and the United States.* Ottawa: 1984.

The Canadian Food Processors Association. "Presentation to the Ministry of International Trade on Bilateral Trade Relations with the United States of America". No date.

Canadian Independent Computer Services Association, "Brief to the Ontario Government Select Committee on Economic Affairs", April 1986.

The Canadian Meat Council. "Comments on Canada's International Meat Trade and Free Trade with the U.S.A." Toronto: June 1985.

The Canadian Textiles Institute. "Submission to the Special Joint Committee on Canada's International Relations re Bilateral Trade with the United States". Ottawa: July 1985.

The Canadian Textiles Institute. "Submission to T.M. Burns, Special Coordinator for Market Access Consultations". August 1985.

Chand, U.K. Ranga. "The Growth of the Service Sector in the Canadian Economy". *Social Indicators Research* 13 (1983) pp. 339-379.

Clairmonts, Frederick F. and John H. Cavanagh. *Transnational Corporations and Services: The Final Frontier.* United Nations: UNCTAD, 1984.

Cohen, Marjorie. "Trade, Free Trade & Statistics". *This Magazine* 20, 3, August-September 1986.

Cohen, Marjorie "Women and Free Trade", in *The Free Trade Papers,* ed. by Duncan Cameron. Toronto: Lorimer, 1986.

Cohen, Marjorie and Daniel Drache. "Politics: The Heart of the Free Trade Debate", in *Un marché, deux sociétés?,* 1ère partie, *Libre-échange et autonomie politique,* eds.: Christian Deblock et Maurice Couture (Montreal: L'ACFAS, 1987), pp. 187-206.

Cohen, Michael and Thomas Morante. "Elimination of Nontariff Barriers to Trade in Services: Recommendations for Future Negotiations", *Law and Policy in International Business* 13, 2, November 1981.

Cox, David and Richard Harris. "A Quantitative Assessment of the Economic Impact on Canada of Sectoral Free Trade with the U.S.". *Canadian Journal of Economics,* August 1986, pp. 377-394.

Daly, Donald J. "Micro Economic Performance: Interrelations between Trade and Industrial Policies". Unpublished paper prepared for the Ontario Economic Council Conference, Canadian Trade at a Crossroads: Options for New International Agreements, April 1985.

Daly, Donald J. "Canadian Manufacturing and International Competition". Paper presented at the Executive Management Forum. Toronto, November 1985.

Daly, Donald J. and D.C. MacCharles. "Persisting Unemployment in Canada –
New Evidence on an Old Theory". Unpublished paper prepared for The
Fraser Institutre, June 1985.

Das, Bhagirath L. "The GATT Multi-Fibre Arrangement". *Journal of World Trade
Law* 17, 2. March-April 1983.

de C. Grey, Rodney. *United States Trade Policy Legislation: A Canadian View.*
Ottawa: Institute for Research on Public Policy, 1982.

de C. Grey, Rodney. *Traded Computer Services: An Analysis of a Proposal for
Canada/U.S.A. Agreement.* Royal Bank.

Deloitte Haskins and Sells Associates, *Canadian Agricultural Trade Issues* Vol.I.
Free Trade with the U.S.A. Toronto, July 1985.

Diebold, William Jr. and Helena Stalson. "Negotiating Issues in International
Services Transactions", in *Trade Policy in the 1980s* ed. by William R. Cline.
Washington D.C.: Institute for International Economics, 1983.

E.C. Commercial Counsellors in Canada. *Trade in Services: E.C./Canada.*
Ottawa, Dec. 1982.

Eger, John M. "Emerging Restrictions on Transnational Data Flows: Privacy
Protection or Non-Tariff Trade Barriers?", *Law and Policy in International
Business* 10, 4 1978.

Elwood, David and Glenn Fine. *The Impact of Right-to-Work Laws on Union
Organization.* Working Paper No. 1116. Cambridge, Mass: National Bureau of
Economic Research, 1983.

Feketekuty, Geza and Kathryn Hauser, "The Impact of Information
Technology on Trade in Services", unpublished paper.

Freeman, Harry L. "U.S.-Canada Free Trade Negotiations: The Importance of
Services", paper presented to Conference on Building a Canadian-American
Free Trade Area sponsored by The Brookings Institution and The Institute
for Research on Public Policy, Feb. 1987.

Friedman, Kenneth J. "The 1980 Canadian Banks and Banking Law Revisions
Act: Competitive Stimulus or Protectionist Barrier?", *Law and Policy in
International Business* 13, 3, 1981.

Fry, Earl H. "Sectoral Free Trade", *International Perspectives.* Sept/Oct 1984.

Fuchs, Victor. *The Service Economy.* New York: Columbia University, 1968.

Gibbs, Murray. "Continuing the International Debate on Services". *Journal of
World Trade Law* 19, 3, May-June 1985.

Ginsberg, Stanley and Robert Hamrin. *Services the New Economy.* Washington:
Coalition of Service Industries, 1985.

Globerman, Stephen. *Cultural Regulation in Canada.* Ottawa: The Institute for
Research on Public Policy, 1983.

Gonick, Cy. *The Great Economic Debate.* Toronto: Lorimer, 1987.

Grocery Products Manufacturers of Canada. "Impact Assessment of Trade
Liberalization with the U.S.", Toronto, August 1985.

Harris, Richard G. "The Economic Impact on Canada of Changing Trade Barriers Between Canada and the United States", paper presented to Brookings Institution Conference on Building a Canadian-American Free Trade Area, Feb. 1987.

Harris, R.G. with D. Cox. *Trade, Industrial Policy and Canadian Manufacturing*. Toronto: Ontario Economic Council, 1983.

Harris, Richard. *Trade, Industrial Policy and International Competition*. Toronto: University of Toronto Press, 1985.

Hart, Michael M. *Canadian Economic Development and the International Trading System Constraints and Opportunities* Vol. 31 *Royal Commission on the Economic Union and Development Prospects for Canada*. Ottawa, 1985.

Hewitt, Garth. "Now the Invisibles Run into Barriers". *International Management* 38 3, March 1983.

Inoussa, Mary C. "Data Processing Services: Managing the Information Explosion", *Business America*, May 13, 1985.

Kirkland, Lane. "Free Trade and Economic Crisis", *The Bulletin of the Department of International Affairs, AFL-CIO*. October 1986.

Laxer, James. *Leap of Faith*. Edmonton: Hurtig, 1986.

Lewis, Russell. *The New Service Society*. London: Longman, 1973.

Lipsey, Richard G. "The Economics of a Canadian-American Free Trade Association", in *The Future on the Table: A Critical Analysis of Canada-U.S. Free Trade Issue*, ed. by Michael Henderson, forthcoming.

Lipsey, Richard G. and Murray G. Smith. *Taking the Initiative: Canada's Trade Options*. Toronto: C.D. Howe Institute, 1985.

Loewen, W.H. "Will Canadian Data Be Processed in Canada?", Unpublished paper prepared for the Canadian Independent Computer Services Association, Winnipeg, October 1985.

Meltz, Noah. "The Female Worker: Occupational Trends in Canada", in *Changing Patterns in Women's Employment*. Ottawa: Women's Bureau, Canadian Department of Labour 1966.

Menzies, Heather. Data Exports: a terminal illness?" *Canadian Business* 54,6 June 1981.

Moroz, Andrew R. "Trading New Services". *Policy Options*, 4,2 March/April, 1983.

Moroz, A.R. and Gregory J. Meridith. *Economic Effects of Trade Liberalization with the U.S.A.: Evidence and Questions*. Ottawa: Institute for Research on Public Policy, Sept. 1985.

Mowlana, Hamid. *International Flow of Information: A Global Report and Analysis*, Report No.99. New York: UNESCO, 1985.

Murray, Grant G. "Trade in Services from a Business Perspective", Address to the Conference Board of Canada, February 18, 1986.

Nelson, Joyce. "Losing it in the Lobby", *This Magazine* 20, 4 October/November 1986.

North-South Institute. *Women in Industry: North-South Connections*. Ottawa, 1984.

North-South Institute. *The Multi-Fibre Arrangement: Unravelling the Costs*. Ottawa, 1985.

OECD. *International Trade in Services: Banking, Identification and Analysis of Obstacles*. Paris, 1984.

OECD. *Monthly Statistics of Foreign Trade*. May, 1985.

OECD. *National Accounts, 1960-1983*. Paris, 1984.

Ontario. Ministry of Labour. *Labour Market Experiences of Workers in Plant Closures: A survey of 21 Cases*. Toronto, May 1984.

Ontario. Ministry of Treasury and Economics. *Ontario Study of the Service Sector*. Toronto: 1986.

Phillips, Paul and Erin Phillips. *Women and Work*. Toronto: James Lorimer, 1983.

Pipe, G. Russell. "International Information Policy: Evolution of Transborder Data Flow Issues", *Telematics and Informatics*, 1.4, 1984.

Reich, Robert B. "Beyond Free Trade", *Foreign Affairs* 61, 4 Spring 1983.

Rotstein, Abraham. *Rebuilding from Within*, Ottawa: Institute for Economic Policy, 1984.

Sawatsky, John. "Inside Dope", *This Magazine*, 20,3 August-September 1986.

Shelp, Ronald Kent. *Beyond Industrialization: Ascendancy of the Global Service Economy*. New York: Praeger, 1981.

Shelp, Ronald Kent. "The Service Economy Gets No Respect", *Across the Board: Conference Board Magazine*, XXI,2, February 1984.

Slofstra, Martin. "AMC plans parent satellite link-up", *Computing Canada*, October 3, 1985.

Spero, Joan Edelman. *The Politics of International Economic Relations*, Third edition. New York: St. Martin's, 1985.

Stanback, Thomas M. Jr., Peter J. Bearse, Thierry J. Noyelle, Robert A Karasek. *Services/The New Economy*. Totowa, N.J.: Allanheld, Osmun & Co., 1981.

Suchman, Peter O. "The Impact of U.S. Federal Laws on Sectoral Integration", *Canada-United States Law Journal*, 10, 1985.

Sykes, Randy. "Privatizing Services", *The Facts* 7, 2 March-April 1985.

Thompson, Fred. "Reducing Barriers to Trade in Nontraded Goods and Services", *Canada-United States Law Journal*, 10 1985.

United Electrical, Radio and Machine Workers of Canada. Presentation to the Select Committee on Economic Affairs, August 26, 1985.

U.S. Department of Commerce International Trade Administration. *Current Development in U.S. International Service Industries*. Washington: March 1980.

Wilkinson, Bruce W. "Canada-U.S. Free Trade and Some Options", *Canadian Public Policy*, VII 1982.

Wilson, S.J. *Women, The Family, and the Economy.* Toronto: McGraw-Hill Ryerson, 1982.

Winham, Gilbert R. *Canada-U.S. Sectoral Trade Study.* Unpublished background paper for the Royal Commission on the Economic Union and Development Prospects for Canada. Ottawa, April 1985.

Wonnocott, Paul. *The United States and Canada: The Quest for Free Trade.* Washington: Institute for International Economics, 1987.

Yeutter, Clayton. Address to the *Chicago Sun Times* Forum, October 1986.

The Network Basics Series

- T.W. Acheson, David Frank, James Frost: *Industrialization and Underdevelopment in the Maritimes, 1880-1930*
- Pat Armstrong et al: *Feminist Marxism or Marxist Feminism: A Debate*
- Howard Buchbinder et al: *Who's On Top: The Politics of Heterosexuality*
- Howard Buchbinder, Janice Newson: *University Means Business*
- Varda Burstyn and Dorothy Smith: *Women, Class, Family and the State;* introduction by Roxana Ng
- Marjorie Cohen: *Free Trade and the Future of Women's Work: Manufacturing and Service Industries*
- Dany Lacombe: *Ideology and Public Policy*
- David Livingstone: *Social Crisis and Schooling*
- Graham Lowe and Herb Northcott: *Under Pressure; a Study of Job Stress*
- Mex Luxton and Harriet Rosenberg: *Through the Kitchen Window: the Politics of Home and Family*
- Roxana Ng: *The Politics of Community Services*
- Leo Panitch and Don Swartz: *From Consent to Coercion: The Assault on the Labour Movement*
- Henry Veltmeyer: *The Canadian Class Structure*
- Henry Veltmeyer: *Canadian Corporate Power*
- Robert White: *Law, Capitalism and the Right to Work*

Garamond Press, 67A Portland Street, Toronto, Ontario, M5V 2M9
(416) 597-0246

Centre Studies

- John Calvert: *Government Ltd.: The Corporate Takeover of the Public Sector in Canada.*
- Don Wells: *Soft Sell: Quality of Working Life Programs and the Productivity Race*

Booklet Series: Please write for complete listing.

- *Alternative Paths to Jobs, Development, Equality and Peace*
- *Working Alternatives*
- *Working Papers for Policy Alternatives*

The Centre is also the Canadian distributor for the World Alternatives Series from the Institute for Policy Studies, Washington.

Canadian Centre for Policy Alternatives, Suite 1004, 251 Laurier Avenue West, Ottawa, Ontario, K1P 5J6
(613) 563-1341

Cohen, Marjorie Griffin

Free trade and the future
of women's work